CONFESSIONS OF AN ORGANIZED HOUSEWIFE

CONFESSIONS OF AN ORGANIZED HOUSEWIFE

by Deniece Schofield

Writer's Digest Books

Cincinnati, Ohio

This book is available at special quantity discounts for sales promotion, premium, fund raising, or educational use.

For details write or telephone Writer's Digest Books, Special Sales, 1507 Dana Ave., Cincinnati, Ohio 45207. (513)531-2222 ext. 246.

94   93   92   91   90   11   10   9   8   7

Library of Congress Cataloging in Publication Data

Schofield, Deniece
   Confessions of an organized housewife.
   Includes index.
    1. Home economics. 2. Housewives — Time management.
I. Title.
TX 147.S36 1982   641.5   82-17458
ISBN 0-89879-100-6

Design by Charleen Catt-Lyon.

CONTENTS

Many people have contributed to this book in many different ways. For this I am immensely grateful.

First is my fantastic husband, Jim, who gave me the enthusiastic support and love I needed to carry out this project. I could never have done it without him.

Our children added many learning experiences to my own education.

My wonderful parents, Fred and Ethel Wheeler, and my brother and sisters have given me a solid foundation for life, on which I draw daily.

My appreciation also goes to all who have attended my workshops, lectures, and seminars. Their questions, ideas, and shared experiences have led to new solutions for many organizational problems.

Introduction

I, Deniece Schofield, being of sound mind and body, must confess that I love housework! But, before you close the book and write me off as a lost cause, let me explain myself.

It hasn't always been this way. I know what it's like to suffer from a chronic case of cluttered closets and negative attitudes.

I knew the principles of organizing. I could even put them to use when I was at work. But at home, life was a series of unwashed dishes, unanswered letters, and unsightly piles of dirty clothes.

I decided to attack the problems head on. I tried and retried various techniques, refined and adapted numerous strategies, and found many new solutions to old home management problems. Soon I was able to handle my housework while enjoying the freedom I needed for other activities.

If you're like me, you not only need motivation to get going; you need to know exactly what to do. This book will do both. It's packed with ideas that will help you take control of your own house.

I can just hear you saying, "There are more important things in life than housework." I agree. However, it is easier to enjoy those "more important things" when you and your family are not burdened with chaos, disarray, and the resulting disharmony. When things are orderly, there is more quality time for whatever your "more important things" are.

I enjoy housework because it helps me get what I want.

Good home management skills provide me with a cheerful background for living. A well-managed home eliminates much tension and irritability. There are fewer interruptions. Because things are orderly, minimal time is spent housecleaning. I have a lot of free time while I still enjoy the benefits of a tidy, comfortable home. From this viewpoint, housework doesn't seem so bad, does it?

TRY IT, YOU'LL LIKE IT

Some time ago I was watching a housecleaning expert on television. After demonstrating several housecleaning shortcuts, he was asked by a member of the studio audience, "What can I do? I just don't like housework. I have a bad attitude." His answer to her was something each of us should know. He said, "The things you like to do, you do well." Just think about it for a minute. If we like housework, we'll do it well. If we don't, we won't. It's that simple.

Now, let's turn his answer around and see what we get. "If you do it well, you'll like housework." Maybe by trying a little harder to do a better job you can gradually begin to like your chores. Step by step, as you improve your household skills, your enjoyment of housework will grow until you, too will be able to say, "I really don't mind housework at all!"

Someone once said that "work without vision is drudgery." What kind of vision do you have? Do you feel depressed and burdened by your domestic responsibilities? Is the only vision you have one of waking to another mess, often finding yourself farther behind than you were the day before?

What you need is to put housework in its proper perspective. View it as a tool to help you get what you want. Don't visualize yourself as a dismal failure. Instead, visualize yourself lying down every night with a peaceful feeling, knowing your work has been done well. You awaken to a house that is in order. The washing has already been sorted and pretreated. The dishwasher (or sink) is empty and you know what you're going to fix for dinner that night. While you are busy with your morning duties, you are rarely interrupted because your family can easily find the things they need.

Sure, things will be spilled and cars won't start. There will still be life's little emergencies and unexpected interruptions. (You may even have some of life's big emergencies!) But even with setbacks, you'll be in better shape than the depressed soul who awakens realizing there is no milk for breakfast; Dad has no clean socks for work; Junior can't find his shoes for school!

I know this from experience, because I have been both of these homemakers. I have felt the thrill of victory and the agony of defeat and I'll take the thrill any day.

THINK GOOD THOUGHTS

You can become a happier, more cheerful you. How? Keep the vision of the "all together" you in your mind. You have to see yourself succeeding before you ever will. If your mind has a positive goal, your body will begin to follow along.

However, as long as you have a negative goal in your mind, you will continue to drift along in a negative manner. The old axiom, "accentuate the positive, eliminate the negative," really pays off in the long run.

Make up your mind right now that it really is possible to become the person in your dreams. Remember, success starts the very minute you do. Put to use some new ideas and you will see your drudgery turn into pleasure. Why? Because after getting things organized you will have so much more time for you!

More than likely, you feel there is a very good reason that you're not as organized as you'd like to be. Because I've had the opportunity to teach and talk to so many people, I think I've heard every excuse in the world! Check to see if yours is included in this list:

"I've got too many kids."

"I have all these preschoolers."

"I have teenagers."

"The kids un-organize faster than I can organize."

"My spouse is a slob."

"I don't have a spouse."

"I have a job outside my home."

"I don't have time."

"I don't have enough money."

"There's not enough storage space in my house."

"I'm always tired. I don't seem to have any energy." (One droopy-eyed woman complained to me, "I'm not a day person and I'm not a night person. My husband wants to know when am I a person?")

While these may be valid reasons for slowing you down, they are not valid enough to stop you. The only thing that can stop you is YOU. There's a U in every excuse. Start substituting action for explanation. Somewhere there's a person with circumstances similar to yours who is organized and efficient. If someone else can do it, so can you!

Recently I read about an older gentleman who, at the age of seventy, was being placed in a convalescent home. He was barely able to walk and care for himself. While this common occurrence hardly seems newsworthy, there's an interesting twist.

Faced with what he considered incarceration, this man looked around and saw people everywhere concerned with physical fitness. He thought, "If they can get into shape, so can I!" He convinced his concerned family to give him one last chance at life before placing him in the home.

His request was granted and he began a supervised physical fitness program. Today, at eighty-two, he is a nine-mile-a-day long-distance runner. He has entered and completed a marathon. He has just written and had published a book that details his accomplishments. All this came from one simple idea that spurred him on: If they can do it, so can I!

So, dump your excuses. You have so much to gain by reaching for your new vision.

As you begin to place the things around you in order, you may very well feel like all your time is being absorbed. Don't give up. Work at getting organized like a hobby. Set aside a certain amount of time each day (or whatever your time budget will allow). While it may indeed take a fair amount of time to establish order, once it is achieved, you will save more time than you have ever spent.

REAPING THE REWARDS

There are so many things I love to do that I'm constantly striving to get more organized so I can have more time to do them. I have my schedule set up so that I have three days a week that require some housecleaning. The other four days are my days off when we simply maintain what's been done. The more efficient I am the more time I have to pursue my particular interests.

Although I consider myself fairly organized, I have days when I set about my work haphazardly, hence my methods are wasteful. By four o'clock on such days I'm usually deciding that the bathroom can wait until tomorrow and I can always wash tonight. On the other hand, if I move systematically and consistently through the house, I can be completely done with everything hours sooner and feel lifted up instead of burdened and defeated.

I point this out for two reasons: First, I know from my own experience that organizing does pay rich rewards in extra time and a fantastic sense of well-being. Second, I also know that even an organized person has days that aren't efficient and well-managed. So, don't be too hard on yourself when you mess up.

If you are an extreme case (we all are, once in a while), try just one new idea at a time. Move to the next idea only when you feel you have mastered the first. Whatever you do, don't throw your dishwater hands in the air and claim disgust, defeat, and insanity! (No matter how efficient I am, though, there are days when even I feel like doing just that!)

Imagine what your home would be like if there were no

complaints from family members. You have the power to make that happen. You can make it so there is nothing for them to complain about.

Often we say, "I have to get out of this house!" Or, "I have to get away!" When I have things running smoothly, our home is the happiest, most peaceful place I know.

Being organized will give you more free time, contribute to a cheerful nature, and add to the peace and security of your home. If you want these conditions badly enough, it is worth all the strength you can muster to work at it. Just remember that the opposite—being overorganized— will make you and your family a miserable conglomeration of nervous wrecks. Efficiency is good only when it works for you, not against you. So, find the level of efficiency that works well for you and use it.

Today more than ever before, we have a wealth of opportunities for development at our fingertips: classes, hobbies, careers, volunteer work—the list is endless. Why should you spend your time trying to find a clean sheet when you can be changing the world?

How to Use This Book

We all have different careers, talents, hobbies, and other demands on our time. However, if the job of home management has fallen to you, then we have one role in common—that of homemaker.

This book is specifically designed to help you master the techniques of hassle-free homemaking.

The book is divided into three sections. The first section, **Work Simplification,** will teach you the very basic principles of organizing. These fundamental laws will help you bring order and organization out of every facet of your life.

Section Two, **Ideas: The Practical Application,** is the exciting thrust of this book. Home management experts are famous for saying, "Have a place for everything and have everything in its place." Then they leave you to your own resources hoping you will figure out a workable solution. Section Two will give you many concrete, specific ideas to try. They will clearly demonstrate how to use the principles you will learn in Section One. Many of the ideas are illustrated to show you what the results of your efforts will be.

The third section, **Getting Started,** will help you do just that! These chapters will help you begin using the principles and application you have learned, and get you over the hump of "getting started."

According to Will Rogers there are three steps to success: (1) Know what you are doing; (2) like what you are doing; and (3) believe in what you are doing. This book will help you fulfill all three requirements.

The work simplification procedures will teach you what to do. The many stimulating ideas you are about to discover will help you like your homemaking role. And, as you get started on your own organizational system, you will see some immediate results. Then, if Will Rogers is right, your success will be guaranteed because it's easy to believe in something when you can see it working.

Just by picking up this book, you have taken the first step on the road to successful home management.

Don't stop now!

PART ONE

Work Simplification

The Basic Organizing Principles

The ultimate purpose of organizing your home and your life is to give you time for more important things. Whether you want to be climbing mountains in Nepal or crocheting afghans, work simplification techniques will give you a clearer path to pursuing your dreams.

On the road to free time you will begin to notice many hidden benefits resulting from your organizational pursuits. You will begin to feel a sense of self-confidence and control over your surroundings. Everyone likes to feel "in charge" of things!

You will experience the exhilaration of finishing the tasks you start. You will see chaos give way to neatness.

If you are bored and unchallenged by home management, you will especially benefit from these work simplification techniques. When you begin seeking out better and faster ways to do your work, you will discover great mental and intellectual challenges (and thus, satisfactions) that will add new zest to any job. Work well done is satisfying and rewarding, but work done without skill leads to frustration and discouragement.

There are a few basic organizational principles common to any endeavor. The president of your bank and the youngster who delivers your newspaper can both benefit from the same methods. You can use them at home and use them again at the office. Work simplification techniques can be used in anything you do. They can even make you a more efficient Boy Scout leader!

Simplicity is the solution to a lot of problems. Here are six easy steps that will bring simplicity out of even difficult circumstances.

THINK BEFORE YOU ACT

This is what being organized is all about: thinking things through logically before you act.

Many people feel that by the time they've finished thinking and planning, they could already have completed the job at hand. Not so! Industrial time and motion experts have estimated that workers are only 50 to 70 percent efficient. Why? Mainly because they work by habit; they act before they think.

Without realizing it, most of us are probably guilty of the same malady, and I am no exception. So many times I tell myself that there is a better way, yet I stumble along falling prey to my old, comfortable habits. For example, when I'm baking something I know I should start with a sink full of hot sudsy water. But, sometimes I say to myself, "Don't waste time doing that—just get busy." When baking time is over, I am faced with a counter full of dirty dishes and little energy to do them. Had I spent two minutes filling the sink, the dishes would have almost done themselves.

Why are we so slow to change? Because as long as we are making it through the day with a fair amount of success, we are satisfied with our performance.

Sometimes it seems easier to keep stumbling along rather than stopping to think. Many times we proceed as we have been taught, thus ignoring other alternatives as to how a job could be accomplished.

When I first set up housekeeping, I put the shoe polish where my mother had stored her shoe polish. I stored my cleaning supplies and food the same way she did. I even folded my towels as she had always folded hers. Lucky for me, Mom knew what she was doing. Had she been a bad example, I would have, unknowingly, accepted her inefficient habits as my own.

Maybe you've heard the story about a young couple who were preparing their Sunday dinner. While he was peeling the potatoes, the husband noticed his wife cutting the end off the ham.

"Why are you cutting the end off the ham?" he asked.

She said simply, "Because my mother always did." Their curiosity aroused, they called Mother and asked why she always cut the end off the ham. "Because *my* mother always did," she answered.

Getting to the bottom of the matter, they called Grandma and asked "Why do you always cut the end off the ham?"

"Because my pan is too small!" replied Grandma.

Think before you act—even before doing routine jobs. The way you perform simple, basic tasks is usually the result of habit, not logical thought.

Until work simplification becomes second nature to you, the thinking and planning process may seem slow. You may feel you are wasting time. But remember, fifteen minutes of planning can save hours.

Over and over I prove the validity of this principle to myself. One day I was in a hurry to pick cherries. My little boy was dressed in nice play clothes, and I didn't want to spend five minutes changing his outfit. So, I snatched him up, put him in the car, and off we went.

When we got home I had to spend twenty-five minutes scrubbing cherry stains out of his clothing. Had I applied the principle of think before you act, I would have spent five minutes changing my son into old clothes and saved myself twenty-five minutes of scrubbing time!

Feodor Dostoevski once wrote, "It seems, in fact, as though the second half of a man's life is made up of nothing but the habits he has accumulated during the first half." That is a distressing statement; but we *can* alter the course of our lives with a little extra effort. We can become aware of time-wasting habits when we think before we act.

DISCARD AND SORT

Of all the work simplification techniques, discard and sort is by far the most important and usually the most difficult! Even if you disregard the other five principles, using this one alone will bring immediate rewards and will simplify your life immensely. If you enjoy this type of activity, here's where you're going to have fun. If this area is a problem for you, I know it can be a difficult and painful experience.

Have you ever said, "There is not enough room in this house!"? The problem is not your house, but your possessions—you probably have too many things. The greatest reward of uncluttering your house will be the time you save getting ready to do a job and cleaning up after the job.

From my consulting work I have learned that those in the worst organizational state are those who have difficulty using the discard and sort technique. Let's explore some ways to make it easier.

Even before you can begin discarding and sorting, you need to determine the function of the room or area in which you are working. For example you may say, "This is the kitchen where I prepare and clean up meals. I serve breakfast and lunch in the kitchen. This is also where pots, pans, and food are kept. Therefore, I do not want to store sheet music, broken bicycle chains, or recycled shoelaces in here." This may seem simplistic, but the principle is important: Determine what function a particular area is going to serve. Then, you can begin to discard and sort.

Work in one area at a time, and keep three boxes and a large trash can with you. One box will hold anything that belongs in another room, e.g., the sheet music, the bicycle chain, and recycled shoelaces. Put things to give away or sell inside the second box. The third box will hold things you're not sure of. The trash basket is there to encourage you to discard everything you possibly can.

FIGHTING FEAR AND SENTIMENT

As you are working in drawers, closets, and cabinets, give every item a hard look and ask yourself the following questions:

1. *Do I really need this?* Fear and sentiment are probably the two main reasons you hang onto things. You're afraid you might need it someday.

To help you overcome your fear, ask yourself, "What is the worst thing that would happen if I got rid of this?" If your house would go into foreclosure, maybe you better keep whatever it is. On the other hand, if nothing drastic would happen, what are you afraid of?

If you're stashing one thing after another, chances are you won't be able to find anything when you need it anyway—so why keep it?

If you have a collection of useless articles (like the ceramic yak Aunt Maude gave you ten years ago) that you're keeping purely for sentimental reasons, remember that things are only symbols of love. Can you keep the love and get rid of the symbol?

2. *How long has it been since I used it?* Things (especially clothing) deteriorate with age. Somehow they never look quite as good as when you first stored them. If you haven't used an item (other than seasonal things) for several months, you probably won't.

3. *Do I need so many?* Duplication of things is especially evident in the kitchen, but look around. Do you really need twenty bottles of nail polish, seven snow shovels, and four extra dog collars? The less you have, the less you have to take care of.

I know there are many dear souls whose hearts yearn for simplicity; but, they can't force themselves to eliminate anything. To you I would say, try giving youself a little pep talk.

Whenever I want to hold on to something I really don't need, I tell myself this: "It is selfish to keep something you are not using. There are many people who would be delighted to have these things." Since I don't like to think of myself as selfish, it works every time. Do you have a friend or favorite charity that needs something you aren't using? Or would a sale entice you? Hold a garage sale, go to a flea market, secondhand shop, or used clothing store. Maybe you could make enough money to buy something you really would use.

If you do find yourself wishing for something you've given away, tell yourself it was a good investment in a clutter-free environment.

Chances are I still haven't convinced you. In that event, set up a central storage area where *all* unused things are kept. That way you will not be cluttering up potentially functional space with unnecessary junk.

Once the sorting process is complete, and to eliminate any temptation, donate or sell the contents of box number two as soon as possible.

Take the third box holding things you are unsure of and put it in a really inconvenient place. A good spot would be the highest shelf in a bedroom closet or the most spider-infested corner of the basement. If something is so important to you that you'll risk life and limb to retrieve it from the box, then that item certainly belongs in your home. If the box sits undisturbed for several months, however, don't you think you can live without those things?

Above all, keep in mind "out of sight, out of mind," and forget the saying, "Absence makes the heart grow fonder."

PREVENTIVE MAINTENANCE

Now you've got your clutter under control. But what's to guarantee that in a couple of years you won't be right back where you were?

Here are a few ideas that will help to prevent the onslaught of junk, stuff, or clutter, whatever you prefer. If you follow these rules faithfully, you may well keep the problem from recurring.

1. Whenever you buy something ask yourself, "Where am I going to put it?" Make sure you have a clearly defined place in mind. Otherwise, you will bring it home and put it somewhere "for now" and the piling process will begin anew.

2. Be certain that you will really use whatever it is you are buying. If you think you'd like to have an electric egg scrambler, borrow one from a friend or relative and try it for awhile to see if you'd really use it if you had one. Maybe, after all, you wouldn't.

3. Keep a running list of things you'd like to buy someday. Chances are, some items will remain on your list so long you'll realize you can live without them. Think before you buy. Your enthusiasm for a particular object often will wane.

4. Learn to say, "No, thanks." Well meaning friends and relatives will often send their castoffs your way. That is great only if you need and will use the things you receive.

5. Ask yourself if the prospective purchase will be time consuming to maintain. If so, are you willing to spend the extra time necessary to keep the article in good condition? My mother always used to complain about ornate furniture and *objets d'art* that to her were dust catchers. Today, I know just what she meant. Do you like or want something badly enough to take care of it? (By the way, I am not referring to your spouse or your children here.)

6. Keep a recycle box handy. Whenever you come across a castoff or other object you're not using, toss it into the box. When the box is full, recycle its contents.

Now you have only the things you need. The next step is deciding what to do with all these necessities. Here's where the next work simplification technique comes in—the principle of grouping.

GROUP

Whenever practical, group and store like items together. For example, have one central location for books and reading material; keep all the suitcases in one place; have one area for toys, and so on. Grouping will trim hours off your housekeeping time.

When you pick up a paperback, let's say, you know immediately where to put it. You (or whoever) won't have to waste time deciding in whose room the book belongs. If you've got several books to put away, you can do it all at once without running from room to room.

When you're setting up a work center, whether in the kitchen, garage, or sewing room, group things together that are used together. This is not as revolutionary as it might sound. As an example, the toothpaste is close to the toothbrushes, laundry detergent is stored close to the washing machine; the iron is near the ironing board, an extension cord is put with portable power tools, etc. This is just common sense and something you are probably doing already. When you're grouping things, ask yourself if each particular object is frequently used in conjunction with another.

The main purpose of grouping is to give everything in your home a well-defined place. If you have a family, this is paramount! Without well-defined, specific places for everything, your family will only have a vague idea of where things belong. They will put things back haphazardly and you'll have to look for them when you need them. Family members need a clear vision in their minds where things belong.

Have you ever noticed what a mess we can make when we're looking for something? Giving things a well-defined place makes it possible to find things before the area is in disarray.

To make the grouping principle more effective, use plenty of drawer dividers. With dividers you have well-defined, well-*confined* places. They help keep the system running smoothly and with less maintenance.

Use drawer dividers in every room in your home. The reason for using drawer dividers in the kitchen is obvious; but, bathroom drawers and dresser drawers can greatly benefit from their use. Use drawer dividers under sinks and on shelves as slide-out trays. You will learn specific ways to use drawer dividers throughout the course of this book.

Keep your bathroom clutter-free
with drawer dividers

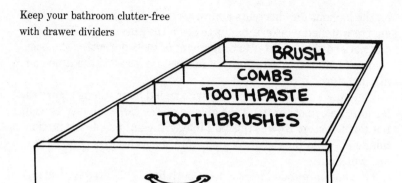

Everything in your house should have such a well-defined place that you could find it in the dark! (The man who lives next door to us claims he can find his socks in the dark and get the right color!) When things do not have a specific place, you become a slave. You are never in control of your house; instead, your house is in control of you.

After trying the grouping principle, a grateful student expressed the following in a letter to me: "I was one of those people who floundered for years looking for answers to the mayhem around me. I definitely wasn't born organized! But now, thanks to you, 'Well-defined, well-confined' is becoming my favorite phrase!"

BE MOTION MINDED

Famous in most home management textbooks is a man by the name of Frederick Winslow Taylor. He was an engineer and efficiency expert who began working for the Midvale Steel Works in Philadelphia in 1878. Big deal, right? Yes! Frederick Winslow Taylor has done more to improve my homemaking skills than any other single person.

Here's how. Taylor conducted experiments to determine how men and machines could work most effectively. He was constantly on the lookout for shortcuts and ways to do things better and faster. He watched workers' hands to see if they used both efficiently and noticed that a better arrangement of tools permitted the best sequence of motion. This part of his system is called the time and motion study.

You may know certain people who spend hours doing a particular job. Yet, another might be able to do the same job just as well, but much faster. How is this possible? Efficient people are motion minded. While they are working, they are conscious of *how* they are working.

The motion-minded person uses both hands effectively. During the next week, notice how many times one hand is busy while one is idle. As an example, what is your left hand doing while your right hand is brushing your teeth? You can easily be sticking things away in a bathroom drawer or medicine chest. Shoulder rests placed on telephones will free both hands for activity during phone calls. Become more aware of your hands.

When you unwrap something do you ever place the wrappings on the counter, only to pick them up and throw them away later? How often do you shuffle through paperwork looking for the bill you need to pay today? Be aware of your motions. Try to handle things only once.

Motion-mindedness doesn't necessarily mean moving fast. It is moving smoothly, steadily, and rhythmically. Of course, moving quickly is the ideal to seek. If you are a right-handed person, your most economical pattern of movement is from left to right. If you are left-handed, the reverse is true. Also, moving in this manner will automatically improve your rhythm and help you work more smoothly.

Here are some specific methods that will help you become motion minded.

1. Store things at or near the point of first use. In other words, store things where you use them. This does not mean that you store the furniture polish on the piano. It does mean that the hot pads are stored close to the oven. This point correlates with the principle of grouping things together that are used together.

In my more disorganized days, all of our electric extension cords were hung neatly in the garage. Because they were all grouped together in an orderly fashion, I assumed I was handling things efficiently. However, every time I sat down to sew, I had to go out to the garage and get an extension cord! When I put the machine away (you guessed it) I was back in the garage replacing the cord. Smart girl. Now, there is an extension cord stored with my sewing machine.

Here's another example. We put our pencil sharpener downstairs close to our main office center. Basically, that was a sound idea. However, when the boys did their homework upstairs in the kitchen they had to run downstairs to sharpen a pencil—moaning all the way. Now, we have another pencil sharpener installed out of sight in the kitchen.

Store things at the point of first use. Here's an often overlooked application of that important rule. Every room in your home needs a trash basket. From time to time, garbage piles up in every room of an average home. So, have a trash receptacle at the point of first use, one in every room.

2. Store equipment and supplies in a way that will allow you to work without having to take a lot of steps. Some people can prepare a whole meal without having to take many steps at all. Still others may walk back and forth across the kitchen many times just fixing a sandwich. (Remember, when you stand in one spot to do something, you're only messing up one spot! The more ground you cover, the more areas you are affecting.)

If you're already employing the preceding principles, this step will follow naturally:

3. Strive for one-motion storage. That means that you can open a cupboard, closet, or drawer, reach in and grab what you want using only one motion. More than likely you have to move things around to get what you need. These extra motions soon add up to a lot of wasted time and energy.

Store frequently used things in such a way that they are easy to see, easy to reach and easy to grasp. As much as possible, store only like items behind each other. Avoid stacking things over two high. (Three maximum.)

One-motion storage is most important for those things you use often. Infrequently used articles can be given two- or three-motion storage, depending on how much you use them.

Do you ever wonder why the kids don't put their clothes in the clothes hamper? Usually, the reason is twofold: first, the hamper is not always at the point of first use; and second, it takes two motions—open the lid and put the clothes in. The more motions something takes, the harder the process is to execute and enforce. Eliminate extra motions and you'll receive better cooperation—even from yourself.

All of us will find those proverbial extra hours in the day by becoming motion-minded. Think before you act. Look at your working motions and equipment arrangements. Find shortcuts through better organization. They could very well turn out to be shortcuts to happiness!

USE YOUR ACCRUED BENEFITS

If you are at all involved with insurance, banking, or real estate you are well aware of what accrued benefits are. *Accrued* means "growing" or "accumulated." An immediate benefit that grows and increases, then, is an accrued benefit.

On the baseball field an accrued benefit is a double play. The defense makes two outs when they normally would get only one.

An accrued benefit at the movies is a double feature. You pay the regular admission and see two movies instead of one.

To a "coupon queen" an accrued benefit is cashing in a coupon for twice its face value. Once again, that's two for one.

Let's discover how accrued benefits can be realized at home. First of all, you need to be aware that every job has three parts: get ready, do the job, and clean up. Frequently, the get ready and clean up take more time than actually doing the job.

For example, your shirt needs a button replaced. So, you get out the sewing basket, look for the right button and thread, sew on the button, and put everything away. (Total time, ten minutes.) The actual sewing used minimal time in this project. Ten minutes time spent on one shirt is excessive. Wouldn't it be better to invest the get ready and clean up in a whole basket of mending rather than only one shirt?

Accrued benefits can be implemented by using one get ready and one clean up time to accomplish as much as possible: doing all the washing; all the tree pruning; all the vacuuming. With today's hectic time schedules it is sometimes impossible to come up with a block of time large enough to complete a whole family's wash or an entire batch of ironing (or whatever). In any case, try to get as much out of one get ready and one clean up as you can.

Another way to accrue benefits is to combine the cleanup of one job with the get ready of another. For example, after breakfast you can prepare what you can for dinner. This way you'll not only have dinner going, you'll be cleaning up dinner preparations while you're cleaning up breakfast. That's two for the price of one.

To aid with the early morning breakfast rush, many people like to set the breakfast table before going to bed. They've used the cleanup from dinner (putting the dishes away) to get ready for breakfast.

You get a wonderful accrued benefit when you straighten the house before bed each night. You've not only completed the day's cleanup, you've done the get ready for tomorrow. That's two for the price of one!

If you get into the habit of replacing things in good condition to their rightful places, you won't have to look for them when it's time to get ready for your next job.

So many times a job is postponed because the get ready time is being spent on something that should have been part of the last cleanup. For example, you can't vacuum until you replace the broken belt; the can of cleanser is empty when you're ready to scrub the bathtub; you have to clean the brush before you can begin painting the house. In other words, get into the habit of completely finishing what you start.

Habits can be wonderful when they work *for* us. Check to see if your habits fall into this category. You may be in the habit of scouring the shower once a week or so. One simple change of habit (wiping the shower down after every use) would eliminate much cleaning time.

Problems are inevitable, but you can prevent and prepare for many of them by looking for accrued benefits.

DO IT DAILY

Once in a home management class I asked each student to write down exactly what she wanted to learn during the course. The results of this survey were very revealing. As it turned out, most of them were there for the same reason: "I want to learn how to get organized so that it will stay that way!" I know of only one place where things magically stay as they are—Never-never Land. Don't expect magic at home.

After all, you can feed your family and in four hours or so they're ready to be fed again. You can comb your hair in the morning, but throughout the day, touchups are required. A few thousand miles after you get your car tuned up it needs another tune up. Every facet of our lives requires attention and maintenance, yet we still seek this state of organized euphoria where *things* stay organized.

Although you can never achieve this impossible goal, you *can* make life much easier by remembering this motto: Do it daily.

Home management needs daily attention. If *everything* in your home is returned to its proper place once a day (or several times a week) things will indeed stay organized. Daily attention requires less time than waiting until the situation is out of control.

Children need to enjoy the benefits of giving their home management duties daily attention. Five or ten minutes a day will keep things in pretty good shape. When we wait until Saturday and say, "Okay you guys, clean your room!" we are usually met with groans and complaints. The children know that a room that's been neglected for a week will take an hour or two to get back to normal. However, if the do-it-daily approach has been used, the children would be enjoying the benefits of a clean room without having to spend a large block of time cleaning.

Maintenance can also solve the problem of "growing" work. The dishes need to be done after every meal. Washed right away, they are easier and less time consuming to clean. You are uplifted and lighthearted having them out of the way. However, if the dishes sit untouched, the job grows and grows. It takes more time and energy to clean encrusted dishes. Irritability builds, recruits are harder to find, and your mood is probably less than genial!

The washing is another good example. Done on a regular and frequent basis, the laundry can be handled in workable portions using small snatches of time. Putting it off causes you to spend a large block of time (which is hard to come by) and creates chaos in the family.

Do it daily is the key to preventing your work from growing.

You already have enough to do. Why add to it with neglect?

THE INDOOR SCOUT

Another motto, taken from the Boy Scouts of America, is "Leave an area better than you found it." I believe that is the Scouts' Outdoor Code. It should become everyone's indoor code.

Whenever I walk into a room and see something out of place, I quickly put it away (or assign someone else to). When I open a drawer or a cupboard and see a misplaced article, I quickly put it in its proper place. It only takes a few seconds to do this. Left undone, it would take fifteen or twenty minutes to redo a drawer. It would take one to two hours to redo an entire room. Spend seconds now and save hours later. Besides, you have more usable storage space when things are kept neat and orderly.

Right now, I imagine you are envisioning me as a compulsive, nervous homemaker who works, works, works from dawn 'til dusk. On the contrary; I am preventing growing chores. Maintaining order is what gives me a lot of free time. After cleaning our home, we all want to protect our investment. Remember, it's much easier to stay on top than it is to catch up.

Do it daily may sound a bit overwhelming to some. Remember that I am not suggesting top to bottom housecleaning every day, just small bare maintenance procedures that will take care of the top layer. If you can't do it daily (or can't delegate it), doing something even three times a week will help. In any case, try to give your home management at least some daily attention.

There you have it—six easy steps to simplify your life: think before you act, discard and sort, group, be motion minded, use accrued benefits, and do it daily.

Now let's look at some practical applications of these principles.

PART TWO

Ideas: The Practical Application

2

Plan Is Not a Four-letter Word

Much of your day goes down the drain, doesn't it? I used to have a lot of days like that. I'd stumble out of bed and fix breakfast. Then I'd slowly work through the house, stopping for an occasional phone call and not-so-occasional interruptions. After lunch I'd leaf through a magazine and later get caught up with curiosity as I wondered which door contestant number one would pick on *Let's Make A Deal*. Soon the kids would come home from school so I'd batten down the hatches and hold on until bedtime. Feeling unsatisfied, unmotivated, and unfulfilled, I awaited a new day.

Almost universally, failure to feel satisfied with our performance or our circumstances can be traced to incomplete planning. Without well-laid plans to give our time direction, we stagger from one thing to the next trying as best we can to handle whatever comes up.

So, let's begin learning to plan completely.

Chances are you already use some planning methods. You probably use a calendar or appointment book at the office. Maybe you even have another one at home. If you're a list maker, more than likely you have little pieces of paper here and there: a grocery list; plans for the high school class reunion; a reminder of an upcoming dinner party with friends. Maybe you use a spiral notebook to jot down miscellaneous tidbits, then search through every page when you need to find something. How about the refrigerator? Is it covered with notes, cartoons, announcements, and messages? Or perhaps your collection is on a bulletin board and you hope nothing important gets buried.

Let's use some of the basic organizing principles we discussed in the first section. What is planning? Simply, it is thinking before you act. Planning is the process by which you coalesce your tasks into a logical pattern. The whole purpose behind this premeditation is to help you get what you want. Whether you want to buy a food processor, build a dog house, or write a book, planning will help you reach your goal in the shortest possible time.

A PLAN WILL SET YOU FREE

Some people fall into time traps when it comes to planning. "I can handle this. No need to waste time planning," they say.

Still others fear that planning takes the fun out of life. One woman told me, "Being organized is okay for some people, but I enjoy living."

A plan does not fence you in. On the contrary! It is your roadmap to freedom. A good plan plots the best course to follow to arrive at your desired destination. A workable plan makes it possible to reach that destination much faster and with much less effort!

To paraphrase Victor Hugo, "When disposal of time is surrendered to chance, chaos soon reigns." There are already enough crises that befall us naturally. Why add to them by failing to plan the things you *can* control?

Planning reduces worry. When things are not written down, you have to keep remembering them so you won't forget. Worry can destroy concentration and lessen the enjoyment you receive from an activity. For example, if you and your friends are having dinner at a nice restaurant, you can't fully enjoy yourself if your mind is humming with things like: "Tomorrow is my mother-in-law's birthday. I can't forget to get her a gift. Don't forget to cancel the dentist appointment. It's my turn to carpool to aerobics tomorrow." When your mind is swimming you can't completely enjoy yourself.

Planning can reduce the number of interruptions that plague you. With a glance at your schedule, you can tell others when you will be available to them. They won't have to keep checking to see if "now" is a good time.

PEOPLE VERSUS PLANS

If you have a particular family member who always demands attention at the wrong time, check your plan. Tell that person when you will be available to read the story or mow the lawn (or whatever), and follow through. I am not proposing that you become inflexible. People are more important than programs, but there are times when you need to judge wisely between the two.

When you sense that another person has an emotional need for your attention, forget your plans. However, there are many times when someone is bored or just wants to socialize. In that case, you need to decide how important your planning timetable is to *you*.

When others see you write down your commitments to them, you are letting them know you won't forget. One of our children tends to be a "reminder" (to put it nicely). His nagging has irritated me more than once. So, I started jotting down my commitments to him (get a birthday present for Benjie, ballgame on Tuesday, money for lunch tickets Wednesday morning). Now both of us are more relaxed. He isn't afraid I'll forget something important and I don't have to be interrupted by constant hints and suggestions. (Occasionally, though, he starts up with, "Don't forget to write it down!")

Here's another plus: Planning keeps your momentum going. Whenever a job is completed, there is usually a feeling of letdown. Checking your written plans can speed you on the way to your next task (or pleasure) before lethargy has a chance to set in.

Here, another basic organizing principle is evident. Without a plan you make many "What should I do next?" decisions throughout the day. A plan lets you decide once. That's an accrued benefit. You have one decision-making time instead of many. You have cut down on indecision and interruptions.

To sum up, planning increases your effectiveness. It helps you see exactly what you have done (where your time has gone) and what is left to do. Planning helps you get the most important things done first; yet, you will still be reminded of smaller jobs that need your attention. Daily planning is the most powerful tool for getting control of your time. Without it you are letting people and events control you.

You may be interested to know that next to inadequate planning, procrastination is the second biggest reason for nonsuccess. So, begin planning now! A plan can help you get what you want. It is your roadmap to freedom. Why wait for success when you can have it now!

3

Take a Look at the Good Book

Let's take planning one step further by adding another work simplification procedure: *grouping*, which is having one central location for things.

All the planning in the world is useless if you can't find your plans. If it takes several minutes searching through a notebook to find your notes, sooner or later you're going to decide, "What's the use?"

A list for this and a list for that is a bothersome method that is doomed to failure. Lists are easily lost, discarded or otherwise destroyed. Psychological theory even claims that the reason people often lose their lists is so they'll have a dandy excuse for doing nothing! Subconsciously, of course!

The system that works is calendaring. A calendar provides you with one central location. You always know where your lists are. No more searching through drawers, bulletin boards, desk spindles, or what have you. A calendar also keeps all necessary information in logical sequence so it is all there when you need it. Your notes and reminders are presented to you in order.

If it's portable a calendar lets you review your future plans whenever and wherever time permits. Thus, your planning is more useful and effective.

Time is your greatest natural resource. It not only deserves attention, it deserves the best equipment. A calendar (preferrably an appointment or engagement book) is all you need.

When choosing a calendar, select one you will enjoy using. While speaking to one particular group, I noticed that several women in the audience had engagement books with mink covers! Now there was a calendar I'm sure they enjoyed using. If your calendar is attractive to you, you will be more likely to use it.

Not only should you choose a calendar by its outward appearance; open it up and flip through it. Notice its format. Common designs are:

Daily—These calendars have an entire page for every day. (Some even use two pages for each day.)

Weekly—This type shows one entire week at a glance.

Monthly—Here you can see one month at a glance.

Notice the layout of the calendar pages. Some are simply large squares or blocks for you to write in. Some have time increments listed like a doctor's appointment book. Some calendar pages have detailed forms with headings, such as *people to see, people to call, correspondence, shopping list, daily menu, expenses, mileage,* etc. If you choose this type, make sure you have something to write in each area so you won't have a lot of wasted space.

If you're not currently using a calendar, you may have to try different styles until you learn what your preference is.

While you are checking the layout, see what else is included in the calendar. Many contain weather maps or charts, lists of payroll deductions, descriptions of monuments in the United States, population sizes of various cities (to name a few). One calendar I saw had articles entitled "Wolves and the Wilderness," "Owning an Island," and "The Bronze Age and the Frescoes." In any case, be sure you're not paying for a lot of things you don't want.

The most useful calendars allow you to add or remove pages. This will eliminate recopying information into a new calendar every year. Also, you can add blank paper for extra notes or other information. For this reason, spiral or bound notebooks are not recommended.

Select a calendar that is large enough to record all the information you need, but small enough to carry with you. Then you will always know your plans. You will be able to give accurate information about your availability when it's needed. How many times have you been asked to do something and had to respond with, "Offhand, I don't know. I'll get back to you"? Keep your calendar with you and you'll always know what you're doing and when you're doing it!

Combine your business, social, and home calendars. After all, your mind functions as one unit. Treat it as one unit. You can't "compartmentalize" your life if you want things to mesh and run smoothly. Use one calendar.

Some families, however, can benefit from using a family calendar, one that is large and hanging in a centrally located spot. Here you indicate business trips, game times, band practices, and the like. This, used in addition to your personal calendar, can keep the entire family well coordinated.

The whole purpose of management, whether in the business world or at home, is to achieve your goals. That is also the purpose of time management. You can begin to reach your goals right now by planning and calendaring. Why wait?

LIVING WITH LISTS

Many people fail to see the need for a calendar, particularly at home. I remember thinking, "Okay, I've got a calendar and I know I should use it. But what do I write in it?" My life, at that point, didn't seem to require calendaring. I thought calendars were only for doctor's appointments, hair appointments, and birthdays. If you feel the same way, you haven't seen the light. Let's explore the possibilities.

I've said all along that planning can help you get what you want. Do you know what you want? It is not my purpose to write a treatise on goals selection, but you need to decide just what it is you want to accomplish with your life.

When you awaken each morning, ask yourself this: "What can I do that will make today meaningful or satisfying for me?" Whether you want to curl up in a hot tub with a good book or go for a ten-mile run, you can use your daily plan to help you get what you want. Once you've answered that question, you've given your day direction. Besides, if you don't know where you're going, how will you know when you get there?

With your goal in sight, list the things you have to accomplish to keep things running smoothly. If you can't decide, jot down whatever comes to mind. Read over the list and check the ones that seem urgent. Are there things on the list that have been bothering you? Do certain entries seem to "jump off" the page?

As you look at each job, ask yourself, "What will happen if I don't do this?" If the answer is, "Nothing," you've indicated a low priority. When the problem is growing, soon to erupt into a crisis, it is a high priority. When the list is narrowed down a bit, try putting the things to do in order of their urgency. Even though there are things I'd rather do, I try to get the "have to" chores out of the way first. That way I can completely relax and enjoy the meaningful objective I have chosen.

Sometimes your goal will be directly related to your priority list. For example, if cleaning out the garage would make the day meaningful to you, your priority list could include related tasks.

When you know what your meaningful objective is, use it as motivation to get going. But, be careful. If you overprogram, you will spend all your time doing other things. Be sure your plans allow time for your goal. And make certain there is room in your schedule to allow for interruptions.

TO THINE OWN LIST BE TRUE

When making your list, be realistic. Determine how much time is available to you and plan accordingly. I know one extremely organized person who is chronically late. Why? Because she has ten things on her list and time to accomplish only seven.

Long lists are discouraging and overwhelming. You will feel energized and motivated after completing a short list; discouraged and defeated by a long list that's half finished.

If the routine jobs on your list bog you down, integrate some stimulating activities throughout:

Quick pickup of house
Read two chapters of new novel
Plant onion sets
Sweep patio
Hot bath—more book
Fold wash

When using your priority list, squeeze in little jobs wherever you can: dust the living room while bacon is frying; water the plants while the bathtub is filling; fold a batch of laundry while watching the news. Keep your eyes open for those accrued benefits.

If you have a large project planned (or imposed), decide how much time it is going to take. Check your calendar and see where you can best fit it in. Schedule it and you will be able to accomplish the job, providing you follow your plan.

KEEP CONTROL

Your calendar can help you say *no* when necessary. A calendar gives you an overall view of what's going on in your life. Sometimes one little request seems harmless, but viewed in relation to the total picture it may be too much for you to handle. A calendar lets you see the overall picture and can help you stay in control.

If you're extremely busy, you may find it necessary to schedule your time off. Guard that time as if it were a doctor's appointment. Some people purposely schedule recreation. Again, they're using a calendar to help them get what they want.

A calendar can even help to unclutter your house. We seem to leave things lying around as a reminder that they need attention. Bills, letters, and announcements are stacked on the counter or desk to jog our memories. "If I leave this pie plate sitting here, I'll remember to return it to Janet." "If I leave this file on my desk, I'll remember to review it before the board meeting."

Use your calendar. Write notes and reminders to yourself as soon as you think of something. Make a note that you need to return the pie plate and put the dish away temporarily. Note the date of the board meeting on your calendar and block out some time to review the file. Then, put the file away. Put away bills, notices, etc. and schedule an office-hours session to handle paper work. Unclutter your house and your mind by writing down the things you need to do. Reread and review your plans frequently to eliminate surprises and get full benefit from your plans.

When your days begin to fill up you might notice that some of the items can be combined or coordinated. For example, you may have an appointment with your lawyer scheduled for four-thirty and a dinner party set for seven that same evening. (You need to pick up bread and dessert at the bakery before they close at six.) The baker and the lawyer are in the same general area, so you can see the lawyer and stop at the bakery on the way home.

Time spent waiting or commuting can be spent planning and reviewing.

After you've used your calendar for several months, note which jobs you are doing over and over. What home management chores keep popping up on your to-do list? Perhaps these are good jobs for you to delegate to a spouse or child. Is there another person who could fulfill that responsibility just as easily?

Maybe these jobs could be broken down into smaller units that enable you to advance a job in small snatches of time rather than one extended work session.

Finally, remember that things will not always run smoothly. The road to success is under construction, and no one is exempt. No matter how well you've planned there will be times when everything seems to go wrong—the car battery will go dead, someone will get sick, a friend will call and need a listening ear. Be determined to accomplish your most important goals, but be flexible. You can put unfinished jobs on tomorrow's list. Sometimes you will need to dearly guard your well-laid plans. Sometimes, other things are more important. Learn to tell the difference.

When faced with choices, try to decide which will accomplish the greater good. Which choice will cause more severe consequences if neglected? In any case, relax and enjoy your life. When it comes right down to it, most things are not life-or-death emergencies!

A COMPLETE PLANNING NOTEBOOK

As a young bride, I was keenly interested in my new job of homemaker. I had a real desire to raise my level of efficiency and have our home run like a well-oiled machine. I knew how to manage an office and I wanted our home to run just as effectively. I read everything I could get my hands on, and tried to absorb as much on-the-job training as I could. Over and over I read about calendaring, listmaking, and setting priorities. I knew that if successful experts relied on calendars, then that is what I needed to do, too.

I went to a nearby discount store and bought my first calendar for $1.50. It was a diary type calendar, with a page for every day of the year. As soon as I brought it home, I noted birthdays, anniversaries, and other important dates on their respective pages. Then, each day I would write the things I had to do, appointments, and our dinner menu.

It all seemed so efficient, and it was, as long as I remembered to use it! For two or three weeks I was the most ardent calendar user in the world. But, after my initial enthusiasm wore off I would lapse and forget to plan my days. Weeks went by with nothing recorded.

I relied heavily on my calendar at the office; I knew its value. Why couldn't I do the same at home? Finally, after starting over many times I developed the habit of recording my plans.

Don't let me discourage you. I hope by exposing my weaknesses you will benefit from my mistakes. Using a calendar isn't that difficult, but it's a habit that needs to be developed. If you are a tough case (like me), just keep starting over until you make it.

One other problem slowed my progress. Sometimes I would forget to look at my plans. I'd leave everything up to memory and hope for the best. Unfortunately, with my memory, that wasn't much to hope for! I would often be surprised by forgotten commitments. Oh yes, I had listed them in my calendar, but I never bothered to check my list.

Gradually, my very own system began to evolve. I started carrying two books with me wherever I went: my calendar and another notebook. The second book contained motivational thoughts and other things I wanted to refer to. This method, however, became cumbersome and violated the grouping principle. So, I decided to combine the calendar and the notebook into one complete planning notebook.

FIRST STEPS

I bought a looseleaf notebook that held 5½x8½-inch paper. This was big enough to record in and small enough to take with me.

Using looseleaf tabs, I divided the notebook into several sections, the first being the calendar section. Inside the front cover of the binder, I taped a small printed calendar of the current and following year. Then, the looseleaf calendar pages were included.

My personal preference was the week-at-a-glance calendar format. I made up my own forms and had them xeroxed. However, you could disassemble a purchased calendar and punch holes in the pages to fit your binder.

The advantage of making your own form is that you get exactly what you want. You can vary the size of the space for each day.

For example, if your Tuesdays are always hectic, make your Tuesday square larger and Wednesday smaller, and so on. I made my Saturday and Sunday spaces smaller because I usually don't have much to record on those days.

I also elected to use another format in addition to the week-at-a-glance. That was the month-at-a-glance. For example, I had January shown a week-at-a-glance. Then I inserted a January month-at-a-glance. Following came February a week-at-a-glance, then the February month, and so on throughout the year.

The purpose of the monthly calendars is to give me a quick overview of any given month. That way I can quickly see if a particular day is occupied without flipping through a lot of daily, week-at-a-glance pages. The daily pages are used for specific details relating to things listed on the monthly squares.

I allow myself plenty of room in each daily square to write my plans and reminders. In the top margin on the left-hand calendar page I print "Highest Priority Tasks This Week." Here I list the main things I want to accomplish that week. Then, as each day is planned, I choose one or two things from my weekly list.

In the top margin on the right-hand side I list errands. By "seeing" all necessary trips, I am able to group things geographically. By plotting just the right course, I can make all necessary stops in one jaunt.

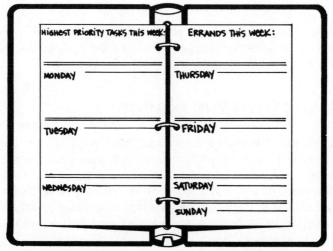

The week-at-a-glance section of a complete planning notebook

I put all those motivational thoughts mentioned previously after the calendar section. Gradually, I realized there were other things I wanted to have with me to refer to, so I inserted other sections. Each was placed behind a labeled tabbed divider.

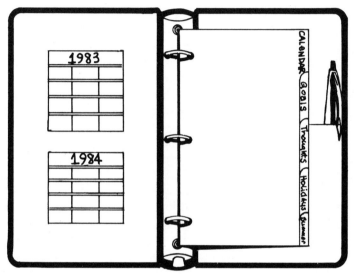

Your complete planning notebook offers total organization

Everything I needed was always at my fingertips. As my life changed, my calendar changed—just by deleting or adding different sections.

DESIGN WITH YOU IN MIND

Purchased calendars are adequate, but if you want just a little bit more from your calendar, a complete planning notebook is the answer.

Many times calendaring fails to work because you're using a calendar that was made for Joe Average Consumer or Jane Children's Dentist. When a system is designed by you with *your* lifestyle in mind, it is naturally more effective and successful. The complete planning notebook gives you those advantages.

Let's stimulate your imagination and look at some creative possibilities for various sections. Keep in mind that I am just tossing out ideas. I am in no way suggesting that you need or should use each one.

Thoughts section is just that. Here I write quotations or motivational thoughts I have read or seen. These are messages that are tailor-made for me. They can motivate me to get going and think positively. Some make me laugh or set me to thinking. They give me a boost on days when I need a lift. Whenever I'm reading or attending a meeting, I jot down quotes or messages I want to remember. I am careful to number each entry so this section won't become a mere hodgepodge of "bits and pieces." (In the chapter on filing, you will see how I have made it possible to find an individual thought or quote.) On days when I'm not up to par, I read my section of thoughts as a source of instant motivation.

A **project** section is useful for listing things you'd like to do someday when you're in the mood. For example: Knit Mother a sweater, make a quilt, refinish the desk. This is the place to write down anything that sparks your interest—a new craft, recipe, or decorating idea.

As you can see, there is no kind of order or sense of urgency here. If you wake up one morning and feel like doing counted cross stitch, you can check your project list to see if there is something you can get going on. Sometimes working with your moods can help you accomplish more than working against them.

Unfortunately, we can't always do what we want to do when we want to do it. Following your mood swings is profitable only when your mood is directly related to something that needs to be accomplished.

Of course, when time permits, it's great to spend hours reading, scuba diving, sleeping, or whatever strikes your fancy!

Whether you're filling out this section of things to do, setting goals, or planning a long-awaited job, remember that you can eat an elephant one bite at a time. So, when listing your projects, break them into bite-size pieces and list each small job in the order it needs to be done.

For example: Make a blue jean quilt for Steven's bed.

1. Gather old jeans.
2. Cut jeans into squares.
3. Buy number 16 sewing machine needle, buy yarn, buy quilt back and quilt batting.
4. Sew squares together.
5. Borrow Judy's quilt frames.
6. Tie quilt.
7. Bind quilt.

This may seem like a lot of work. It may even seem a little foolish. But the purpose is to make any project seem less formidable. Bite-size pieces are easier to swallow. Making a quilt seems like a monster looming on the horizon. But buying a sewing machine needle and yarn isn't so bad. Cutting quilt blocks isn't too hard. Gradually and almost painlessly, you will be led to the completion of your goal.

By listing all the mini steps, you will be able to get a handle on many long-overdue projects. It is important that you be able to finish one step in a single day. Long projects are easy to put off because they lack immediate rewards. Simple steps, easily completed, keep the rewards coming and keep you moving toward your goal. As you proceed from one step to another you will find there is something very motivating about crossing things off your list.

A **housecleaning** section for the planning notebook is also helpful. Here you list your housecleaning schedule. This will be discussed in detail in the following chapter.

A **purchase** section can be a real money saver and clutter preventer. In this section you list things you'd like to have someday (a microwave, ice cream dishes, a filing cabinet, new kitchen shears, etc.). This section can be useful in many ways.

First, it can save you money by reducing impulse purchases. I remember years ago I wanted to buy some small ice cream dishes. Oh, how I wanted those dishes! I recall how I used to imagine myself serving mouth-watering desserts in them. I quickly gave way to my determination and bought the dishes. Today, they are sitting neglected and unused on a kitchen shelf, the product of an impulsive purchase.

When you think you can't live without something, list it in your purchase section. Give your enthusiasm a chance to fade. Maybe your mood will swing and you'll decide against it. Not only will you save money, you will save your house from more clutter.

The list in your purchase section can also motivate you to begin a savings or budget program that will allow you to pay cash for a desired article. That will also save you money. In the purchase section you may also want to record the budget program you're setting up to help you save for a wanted item.

Use the purchase section to help eliminate some of life's little irritations. As an example, one of our children always had wrappers and trash lying on his dresser, stuffed in his sock drawer, and any other convenient place. I decided what he needed was a trash basket in his room. I listed it in purchase section and as soon as I had a few extra dollars I bought one for him.

Whenever you have a little extra cash, glance down the list and see if the money could be used or saved for one of the items. If money is not given direction, it soon goes a dollar here, a dollar there with nothing to show for it.

A **menu selection** section will help if you spent the first twenty years of your life wondering who you'd marry and the next twenty years wondering what to have for dinner. These menu selection sheets will be discussed in detail in one of the following chapters.

A **holiday** section can keep you celebrating if you celebrate holidays in a big way. Whenever you see a cute decorating idea, read a delicious sounding holiday recipe, or hear about a clever tradition, jot it down in the holiday section. If you've seen a craft pattern for something you'd like to make, note where you saw the directions. This is also a good place to note what supplies you have leftover from the previous holiday (six rolls of Christmas wrapping paper, three Pilgrim candles, four New Year's Eve horns). Then, when the holiday rolls around you won't have to remember what's being stored. You will be able to purchase accurately.

A **summer** section is useful to the busy stay-at-home parent wondering how to get through the summer. During the winter, start making notes of various ideas: arts and crafts projects, places to visit, educational ideas, cooking and baking projects, a list of good books. In late spring, sit down with all your notes and start making some plans. Set aside some time each week to do a few of these things. Summer will be less frantic for you and less boring for the children when you have a few structured activities.

An **odd jobs** section is another idea. Here you indicate home repairs and yard work (caulk the shower, repair wallpaper, fertilize the lawn). Nagging is quieter on paper, by the way, if you're planning to pass this list along to another family member. This is an ongoing list.

A **medical history** section might also be useful. List names and birthdates of family members, health history, and immunization records. This section could also be used for pet records.

A **personal data** section could help with the many numbers we have to keep track of: social security numbers, bank card numbers, name of bank, type of account and account number, safety deposit number, credit card information (company name, number, expiration date, whom to notify if you lose the card), driver's license number and passport number. Other things to include might be: auto information (make of car, insurance company, amount, policy number, location of policy, expiration date, license number, serial number, registration number, title number). Boat or trailer information (motor serial number, model serial number).

Insurance policies of all types could be listed. (Company name, agent's name and phone number, policy type, policy number, amount, location of policy, expiration or conversion date.)

Would a list of expiration dates on mortgages, certificates of deposit, bonds, etc. be helpful to you?

A **household** section lists room sizes, paint colors and numbers, window and bed sizes, wallpaper swatches, etc. If you're out shopping and see something you might like for your home, you'll have all the necessary information with you. This section has obvious benefits if you've moved recently or are remodeling.

A **family** section keeps track of sizes, measurements, and ideas for gifts. This is especially helpful with grandchildren or when other family members are living away from home.

A **financial** section is used to record mileage, meals, and other business expenses. Various household expenses are also recorded here (food and clothing expenditures, for example). Having your planning notebook with you gives you a convenient place to record this information. Jot down these expense items right on the daily squares for easy access.

A **birthday** section could be another heading. Use a page or half page for every month and list all the respective birthdays. You'll never again have to transfer birthdates to your calendar.

Finally, consider having temporary sections: vacation plans, including a list of things to pack; information for an upcoming business trip; plans for a special party; preparations for going away to college; wedding plans; plans for the club luncheon.

You see? Your complete planning notebook is limited only by your imagination. Begin by setting up a calendar section and let the rest of your planning notebook evolve naturally. As you discover different things you'd like to have with you to refer to and use, add a section to your book. (Every time I stopped into the library or browsed through a bookstore, I wished I had remembered to bring the list of books I was trying to locate. Thus, my book section was born.) My notebook is the glue that holds me together. I know it will do the same for you!

4

A House That's Always Clean

We all hear it—usually about other people. "Oh, their house is always clean." Then we cringe a little inside wishing that it were *our* house they were talking about.

Well, just to set the record straight, there is no such thing as a house that's always clean! Even a house with no occupants gets dirty. Yet there is something in our psyche that tells us "a house that is always clean is my goal." That one little idea causes us so much discouragement. We need to realize that no matter who "they" are, or how they clean, their house is sometimes a mess.

We must stop comparing ourselves with other people. I am five feet seven inches tall. Because my sister is six feet, does that mean I am short? Certainly not! It simply means that we are different.

I have five children who eat in the kitchen every day. As a result, I usually have to wipe up the floor on a daily basis. My friend, with no children, wipes up her floor once a week. Does that mean I am cleaner than she is? Absolutely not! Circumstances and lifestyles vary too much to make comparisons accurate. The only effective measuring stick is to compare where you are today with where you were six months ago! Don't ever compare yourself to anyone else.

We tend to see *our*selves at our worst, while we see others at their best. When you walk into a neighbor's house, you see a shining entry way and formal living room. Automatically, you assume their entire house is in the same condition. Then your mind flashes back to the state of your own house. Maybe your entry and living room are showplace perfect, too, but all you can visualize is the sorted laundry lying in front of the washer. You remember the fingerprints on the sliding glass door and immediately you feel inferior to your friend. You jump to the conclusion that he or she is a better manager than you are! How someone else's home looks simply does not matter. What does matter is that we have a happy, comfortable home.

THE SCIENCE OF HOMEMAKING

However, a certain semblance of order and hygiene is required. The only way to keep things going (and to keep your name out of the paper—I'm sure you've read articles about the filth the health department found at such and such an address)—is through the labor of housework.

Outcries against housework are becoming more and more common: "It is boring; it is unfulfilling; it is monotonous; it is never done. I hate to do over today what I didn't even want to do yesterday."

The reason we feel this way is that we take on home management with little or no training. We have to learn through experience, through trial and error. No wonder housework becomes a drudge!

Using the basic organizing principles we discussed in the first section, you can learn to simplify housework so it takes less time and energy and becomes less of a drudge. You will then be free to do more important things. Using these principles you can schedule your work conveniently. Your improved attitude may very well attract other family members so they will then begin to consider home management a science, not just "women's work"!

Remember, the very first step is to *think before you act*. One of the reasons housework seems unfulfilling is that our methods are often inefficient and wasteful. Plan your work, looking for better ways to accomplish it. That alone will raise housekeeping from the mundane and put it into the scientific class. And your work will become more fulfilling and challenging.

Before we go on vacation, we decide on a destination, then we decide how we will get there and what route we will take. Scheduling your work is like planning a trip. It gives you a destination and serves as a roadmap for your journey. I'm sure you can appreciate the value of vacation itinerary, but how often do you journey through your day's work without direction?

Specifically, why do YOU need a schedule? If you are a slob, you need to know that you have to do something. You need to know that you have to start. You need to see in writing what has to be done and when. A schedule will at least help you do better than you're doing now!

If you're a perfectionist, you need to know when to stop. You need to realize there are more important things in life than housework.

Being a perfectionist is extremely inefficient. Let me give you three real-life examples. Perhaps seeing this will help you see the folly of your ways.

I am personally acquainted with three perfectionists. One of them irons shoe laces. The second one scrubs the garage floor with bleach once a week. The third misguided soul changes the sheets on her son's bed once a week. Now, if that boy were still living at home, changing his sheets once a week would seem reasonable. But, he's been married and gone for three years now!

WHAT PRICE PERFECTION?

What is your perfectionism costing *you?* Time, mostly, but you are paying other prices as well. You can stifle creativity by providing too sterile an environment. One man I know has a perfection problem. On several occasions his children have set up a game and gone back to the toy room to get a missing piece. While they were gone, he'd quickly put the game away.

You can make people feel uncomfortable and unwelcome when they're allowed to walk or sit *only* on plastic. Your desire for perfection is also costly to your nervous system. You've probably heard about the woman who goes to bed with string mops attached to both feet. That way, if she has to get up during the night, she can be accomplishing something!

If you see yourself in these examples, learn to relax and try to do one job imperfectly every day. You will save hours just by changing your standards. Life is too short to worry about yellow wax buildup.

Now, if you fall into neither category, maybe you're the "I just can't stick to a schedule" type. That's fine, but you need a schedule, too. People in this group usually fear being entrapped. If that is the case, approach your schedule like this: "I am not going to follow this schedule, but I can choose three jobs and do those." Or, "I can follow this schedule for half a day, then I'm free." Used in this way, a schedule can serve as a guide, reminding you of jobs that haven't been done for a while and helping you remember the ones that have. Once you begin to see how a schedule can bring you more free time, it will become increasingly useful to you.

Next, there's always the group who says: "I can see when the piano needs dusting. What do I need a schedule for?" You may very well be operating on a mental schedule without even knowing it.

Schedules help you form good habits and get you into a smooth routine. With a schedule things are kept up on a regular basis without suffering serious neglect. If you're accomplishing these ends, you've got a schedule, all right. It's just written in your head, not on paper. But if you do find things neglected and out of control now and then, a written schedule might be in order.

VISIBLE BENEFITS

Scheduling can save a great deal of getting ready and cleaning up time. For example—to set up the ironing board, heat the iron, and put everything away when finished takes about five minutes. I can iron a shirt in six minutes. So if I iron a shirt every time I need one, it will take eleven minutes for one shirt. However, if I schedule an ironing day and do all the ironing at once, I can save an enormous amount of time by getting ready and cleaning up *once*, instead of many times.

The total time spent ironing five shirts at one time would be as follows:
Setting up/putting away.........................5 minutes
Ironing five shirts (six minutes each) ....30 minutes
TOTAL TIME SPENT........................35 minutes

The total time spent ironing five shirts at different times, or as needed would be as follows:
Setting up/putting away........................25 minutes
(five minutes each time)

Iron five shirts (six minutes each) . . . . .30 minutes
TOTAL TIME SPENT. . . . . .55 minutes

You can see from this example that scheduling ironing time can save a total of twenty minutes. That may not seem dramatic, until you figure that twenty minutes a week is seventeen and one-third hours a year. I can think of a lot of ways I would like to spend those hours—and setting up and taking down the ironing board is not one of them! Having and following a schedule is well worth your time. Remember, *planned time means more time!*

When you rely on a housekeeping schedule you don't have to stop to figure out what you're going to do next. You can keep your momentum. Stopping every so often to make decisions is time consuming and energy depleting. You conserve your energy when you cut down on indecision. You can perform routine tasks almost automatically.

A schedule keeps you from doing some jobs more often than is necessary. You don't forget a job that might go undone.

The main reason for having a housekeeping schedule is that it gives you a sense of completion. Housework is never done, but with a schedule, *you* can be. Monday's work can be finished. Tuesday's work completed, and so on. Even though some areas of the house are undone, you can relax and say, "That's Thursday's work." Without a schedule you always feel snowed under, trying to catch up. Enjoy the exhilarating feeling you get when something is finished.

5

A Schedule Made for You

Often I hear, "Oh, I tried your schedule (or so-and-so's) and it just didn't work!" Of course it didn't work. Schedules are very personal and individual things. They should reflect your lifestyle, your energy level, the size of your family, the amount of help you have, and how many hours you're able to be at home.

Whenever you see a housekeeping schedule in a book or magazine go ahead and read it, but don't accept it as if it were scripture. Notice how it is set up. Read through the list of jobs and see if it gives you any ideas. Be objective when doing this and don't automatically conclude that there is one right method, or that yours is inferior.

Schedules are sometimes set up idealistically. Make certain that your schedule has reachable goals. That way, you will have built-in success. Schedules are not carved in stone, they are written on paper. They need to be modified and changed as your life circumstances dictate. If you decide to go back to work, your schedule will need revamping. The birth of a baby will require many schedule alterations. Relax and let your schedule help you get what you want.

Sometimes a schedule becomes so involved with trivia that important jobs are overlooked. When that happens, the system ceases to function.

After a class or a lecture, people will say to me, "I am the worst organizer! I haven't scrubbed the tile grout (with a toothpick) for three weeks!" If your schedule calls for tedious and frequent tile grout scrubbings, then you're overconcerned with trivia. Make sure priorities are built into your schedule. Here are a few guidelines. No matter the size or shape of your home, or the number of occupants, there are certain bare essentials that must be done first. They are:

1. General pickup of the house including making beds.
2. Laundry kept current.
3. Well-balanced meals served regularly.
4. Dishes done frequently.
5. Bathrooms cleaned and straightened regularly.
6. Entry areas clean and neat appearing. (This is to avoid embarrassment when the doorbell rings. It is not necessary for the well-being of the family, but it will help your peace of mind.)

When time is tight, just doing these basic jobs will be enough to see you through.

MAKING YOUR OWN SCHEDULE

With these directives in mind, let's make a tailor-made-for-you schedule. Simply take the following steps:

1. Before you can begin scheduling, determine first of all how much time you can or want to spend cleaning. Placing your schedule within certain time restrictions will keep you from overprogramming or from scheduling nonessentials. My schedule is set up something like this:

Monday—Clean (two hours)
Tuesday—Maintain (minimal time)
Wednesday—Clean (two hours)
Thursday—Maintain (minimal time)
Friday—Clean (three hours)
Saturday—Maintain (minimal time)
Sunday—Maintain (minimal time)

To help you understand my cleaning rationale, I have a husband, five children and a medium-sized house. Also, I am home most of every day.

How many days (or hours) do you want to clean? How many days can you maintain? Once you have a schedule "roughed in" you can begin making specific plans.

2. One by one, go through every room in your house. On a sheet of paper list everything you think needs to be done to thoroughly clean that room. Remember, this is according to you! How clean do

you think the room needs to be?

3. Next, decide how often you think the job needs to be done—daily, weekly, monthly, or seasonally, and note your decision by each particular job.

There is no right standard here. For example, a family with several small children and only one bathroom will need to clean the bathroom daily. A single person living in a condo with two bathrooms could easily get by with a weekly cleaning. Daily dusting may seem excessive to some and necessary to others. A very pale or dark-colored carpet will need more frequent vacuuming than a variegated carpet.

You see how a schedule needs to reflect your lifestyle and physical surroundings?

4. Decide (and note) who is responsible for each specific job.

After you have made these decisions, chart your plan onto a permanent list. I keep my schedule in the cleaning section of my planning notebook. However, some people prefer to keep their lists on index cards or large posters. Choose any method you like. The important thing is to have a system that you will use. A sample of my own housecleaning schedule can be found at the end of this chapter.

Until you have your schedule memorized, you will have to refer to your chart every day. You may want to list all your daily chores each day on your daily calendar pages. Whatever works best, try to be faithful. You will see an improvement in your house and your attitude.

Recently, I got a letter from a woman who shared with me the joy she has experienced from scheduling and getting things under control. She says, "I am no longer afraid when my mother comes over! What freedom! What joy! She called and said she was coming and I panicked, as usual. I started to rush through the house, madly cleaning, but there was nothing to trim up, nothing to clean!

"The same thing happens when my doorbell rings. I no longer lock my children and myself in the bathroom in silence, waiting for the callers to leave. (Or, red-faced, let them in while kicking dirty socks out of the path.)

"Now I can't believe I ever lived the way I did before. Thank you for sharing self-respect, pride, and *time*—not to mention the relief to my stomach!"

DENIECE SCHOFIELD'S HOUSECLEANING AND HOME MANAGEMENT SCHEDULE

DAILY

- Pickup; dust; make beds; wipe up kitchen floor; clean kitchen, including sliding glass door, sink window, and telephone.

- Vacuum thoroughly Monday, Wednesday, and Friday. As needed on Tuesday, Thursday, and Saturday.

- Laundry on Monday, Wednesday, Friday, and Saturday.

- Bathrooms cleaned thoroughly Monday, Wednesday, and Friday. Straightened and wiped up on Tuesday, Thursday, and Saturday.

WEEKLY

- Monday—iron, mend, clean fireplace.

- Tuesday—paperwork.

- Wednesday—water and dust plants.

- Friday—wash sheets and bedding as needed; scrub rock entrance; wipe doorknobs and light switches; wash front door; polish kitchen canisters and cupboards; wash trash baskets; scrub kitchen floor (wax as needed); shop.

- Saturday—clean garage.

BIMONTHLY

These chores are broken down by room. They are done during the last two weeks of January, March, May, July, September, and November. These bimonthly chores are done in addition to the daily and weekly jobs outlined above.

In All Rooms: Vacuum furniture, window tracks, floor edges, register vents, underneath furniture; wash windows, blinds, and woodwork; dust ledges and baseboards, pictures and frames; remove cobwebs; clean decorations and light fixtures.

Living Room: Dust inside of piano.

Family Room: Vacuum and straighten toy closet.

Bedrooms: Vacuum mattresses; dust and straighten shelves, straighten drawers.

Kitchen: Vacuum sliding glass door tracks; straighten, wash, and polish cupboards; clean oven hood, oven, and refrigerator; clean under oven and refrigerator; straighten and clean utility closet; empty vacuum bag, or as needed.

Bathrooms: Scour shower; straighten and clean drawer dividers, drawers and shelves.

Hall and Entry: Straighten and vacuum linen closet and entry closet; wash hand rails.

Laundry Room and Office Area: Straighten and dust shelves and closet; vacuum dryer and clean washer; clean floor as needed; vacuum water softener, furnace, and hot water heater.

Semiannual: These can be done in conjunction with monthly chores in March and September.

Clean or air drapes; wash blinds; wash walls, ceilings, closets; polish paneling; vacuum storage area under stairs; shine plants; turn mattresses; thoroughly wash cupboards and shelves.

Note: There are times when I don't have a two-week block of time to get my deep cleaning schedule completed. In that event, I simply deep clean one room a week using this schedule as a guide. That way, I spend less time per day cleaning. However, it takes about ten weeks to finish the entire house. perhaps this is not the ideal way to do it, but it's better than doing nothing and a good alternative when time is tight.

6

Get Set

The success of my housecleaning schedule starts the night before. In the evening I go through the house and put things in order, rounding up any volunteers. I don't clean, I just pick up and put away. If possible, I empty the dishwasher. I have found that when I wake up to an empty or nearly empty dishwasher, my spirits are lifted. In other words—*don't start today by doing yesterday's work.*

Planning tonight what you're going to do tomorrow gives you a head start. For example, if cleaning the oven is scheduled, you can soak the stove drip pans, burner rims and oven racks in an ammonia solution all night. That will sure save you scrubbing time in the morning.

One industrious woman gets a head start by thoroughly cleaning her kitchen after dinner. She says her husband is unwinding and doesn't need her right then, and her children are usually occupied during that time. She has found that she would rather do her kitchen in the evening than use her valuable morning time.

Now that we're all set for tomorrow, we can lie down in bed like the person in our vision. We can experience that same peaceful feeling because we know our work has been done well and we are prepared for tomorrow. Ahhhhh, sweet dreams.

GO LIKE A PRO

All too soon it's time to arise and face another day. Even though we are not often treated like professionals, we need to get up and handle our jobs professionally.

When you have a job outside your home, you know the necessity of rising early and preparing for a day at work. We need this same professional approach at home. On my busier days (Monday, Wednesday, and Friday especially) I try to get up at five or six in the morning. I am always amazed at how much I can get done before seven. There are no interruptions.

Once when I was telling a friend about my plan, she said, "What do you *do* at five in the morning?" Here are a few ideas. I can wash, iron, mend, file, write letters, read, exercise, plan menus, choose new recipes, note progress and update goals, do sewing and craft projects, and I can clean the downstairs. These jobs are such that I won't disturb any sleeping people.

If you can't drag yourself out of bed that early, at least try to get up before your children do. Children seem to have so much energy and if we can get a head start on them, so much the better. When they're doing tribal dances around your bed, begging for breakfast, they are beginning to control your day. How much better to be awake and ready for them so you'll be in control and operating on *your* terms.

Dressing and acting the part of a housekeeping pro will help us speed through our work. Even though people on television clean house in chiffon evening dresses and Farrah washable suits, dress in loose, comfortable, and appropriate clothes. Although you won't look like you're ready for a night on the town, have yourself looking neat and presentable. If you feel good about the way you look, your attitude and disposition will improve. Also, if your state congressional representative comes to the door soliciting votes, you won't have to hide your appearance by talking through a cracked open door!

Watch professionals for ideas. When someone makes a living doing a certain job, he usually has the tools and knowledge of his trade to help him work efficiently. Notice their work simplification methods. Pay attention not only to how they *use* their equipment but see now it is *stored*. You'll get many fresh insights that will spark new ideas for you to use at home.

For example, have you ever seen a busboy clear a restaurant table? He loads everything into a big dishpan and heads for the kitchen. The table is completely cleaned off *in one trip*. We can do the same thing. When setting the table, carry everything to the table in a clean dishpan. After dinner, put everything back into the dishpan and head for the sink.

With a cleaning cart it's easy to take a professional approach to housekeeping

USE A UTILITY CART

Watch professionals who have jobs similar to yours. They know the best and fastest ways to do things. Here's another example:

Have you ever watched a hotel maid sweep effortlessly through her duties? She has everything she needs on her cart and avoids chasing back and forth for things. She moves around the room in a circle and eliminates unnecessary steps. I always wanted a smaller version of a cart like that, but I had no place to store one. I didn't give up, though, because I really wanted one. Well, a simple shopping cart (sometimes called a utility cart) proved to be just right.

If you don't know what a shopping cart is (not to be confused with a grocery-store shopping cart) you need to think back a few years before we were all two-car families. Remember when Mom or Grandma walked to the grocery store wheeling a little cart? After shopping, she would load up her cart and walk home pushing her purchases along. We don't see these little carts much anymore, but they are still on the market.

Only a few adaptions are needed to make the cart serve as a utility cart. A dishpan or clean-up caddy sits on top to hold cleaning supplies and rags; or, hang a bucket or plastic ice-cream pail on the side. I have sewn two large bags that hang on each side of the cart. Some of my students have purchased heavy laundry bags and secured them to the cart.

Like the professional maid, I move systematically through the house. When I begin cleaning, I wheel the cart into a room and remove the dishpan full of cleaning supplies. All soiled laundry is put into the cart. Trash is put into one bag, and things that belong in another room are put into the second bag. When the room is cleaned, I replace the dishpan and wheel the cart into the next room.

Having a bag for misplaced articles keeps you in the room you're working in. How many times have you left the room you were working in to put something away and said to yourself, "While I'm in this room, I'll . . . "? Before you know it, you're completely sidetracked from your original job!

Before my cart days, I would frequently clean like this: enter the bedroom with cleaning supplies (if I remembered them), pick up soiled laundry, walk down the hall to the hamper, notice that towels are lying on the bathroom floor, refold towels and put them away, see a bit of mud on the floor, go to kitchen for a rag, rags in dryer, go downstairs to get a rag, may as well fold a batch of clothes, and so on.

Now you can see how many steps and *how much time* I save moving systematically. As I enter a different room, I go through the second bag and remove all the things that belong is that room, then continue as before. When my work is finished, I return the cleaning supplies to the utility closet, deposit all the laundry in the hamper and empty the trash bag. The cart completely folds up and is easily stored away.

The cart can also be used as a laundry cart. Folded clothes can be placed in the cart and wheeled from room to room as you put them away. So think like a pro and act like a pro. You'll be able to handle any household chore that may come your way.

FOR MORE ADVICE

As I'm sure you've noticed, the thrust of this book is order—how to organize your tasks and your possessions, where to put things, and so on. Many people, however, have asked me for specific cleaning advice such as how to clean walls, windows, and carpets. I always refer them to a professional!

For an in-depth approach to housecleaning, I strongly recommend three books by Don Aslett (owner of Varsity Contractors, a multi-million dollar cleaning business): *Is There Life After Housework?*, *Do I Dust or Vacuum First?*, and *Clutter's Last Stand* (Writer's Digest Books). Aslett's entertaining and extremely informative material is all you need for a complete how-to-clean guide!

AN OUNCE OF PREVENTION

After investing your valuable time in a clean house, protect your investment. Avoid the tendency to be a "for now" person. "I'll just set this book on the dresser for now." Or, "You can put those things on top of the refrigerator for now." Sound familiar? The "for nows" soon become "forevers" and before you know it you're spending hours cleaning house!

Every time I go into a room, I quickly put back anything that is out of place (or I assign someone else to). When I open a drawer and see something out of place I quickly put it in order. It only takes a few seconds to do this. Remember that it's a lot easier to stay on top than it is to catch up. After all, if you don't have time to do it right the first time, when will you have time to do it over?

Once I've cleaned, *maintaining* order is what enables me to take four days a week off. My goal is to have everything in the house put back where it belongs by the end of the day. That way nothing gets in too desperate a condition. Even though I follow a schedule and try to maintain order, I am not a slave to my house, because I stay in control of the situation.

No, there is no such thing as a house that's *always* clean. You will feel a great sense of accomplishment and satisfaction. Then, all those good feelings will spill over as motivation for the next day.

7

The Four Storage Alternatives

Did you know that about 10 percent of the space in your home or apartment is needed for storage? That means, if you have a two thousand-square-foot home, you need two hundred square feet of storage space available to you. How does your storage space stack up? (Pun intended.)

Many of us complain that we do not have enough room for storage. More than likely, we either have too many things or we have not used our existing space efficiently.

Before adding any new storage areas to your home, be sure that you have eliminated unnecessary belongings. Organize the space you have before you undertake any major building projects.

Remember the law of the home: Junk expands to fill the space available, plus one room. More storage space may just give you more space in which to be disorganized.

We are all bound, to some degree, by the architecture of our living quarters. A particular article may seem best suited to drawer storage, but when you have no drawer space you must start using your imagination!

There are only four storage alternatives. You can either **hang** things up, store them in a **drawer,** on a **shelf,** or put them on the **floor.** If drawer storage, for example, is not possible, ask yourself if the item can be hung, put on a shelf, or stored on the floor in some manner.

No matter what storage problem you are faced with, you can find your best storage alternative by looking at these four possibilities. Oftentimes, you can work around the existing architecture of your home and save the many hours and dollars of a remodeling project.

Next time you hear yourself saying, "Now, what am I going to do with *this?*" stop and think. Then ask yourself, "Of the four storage alternatives (floor, drawer, shelf, hanging) which one would work best for me?"

In the chapters that follow, you will learn how to physically organize the space around you. To give you a stronger foundation on which to build, let's examine each storage alternative in detail.

HANG IT UP

Here, you have a variety of possibilities. Kitchen utensils are easily adaptable to hanging. Most restaurant kitchens store things in this manner, so it must be an efficient method.

Items can be hung on pegboard or out of sight on the inside of cupboard doors. Hang most frequently used items by your mixing center and save steps in preparing meals.

In the kitchen and bathroom, look under your sinks. There is a lot of wasted space there! Stock up buckets or plastic ice cream pails with extra or seldom used things and hang them on a nail. They're out of sight, out of your way, and still accessible when you need them.

There are many commercial products designed to help you hang anything from paper sacks to the ironing board. Even metal parts cabinets (the kind with all the little plastic drawers) can be hung up. If you're unaware of the products available, walk through the housewares and hardware departments in all of your favorite stores. Check industrial or business supply catalogs. Acquaint yourself with the variety of storage helpers you can purchase.

Bats, rackets, and other sports equipment can be hung on pegboard or secured between two closely placed nails. Stored in this way they are safe, visible, easy to find, and easy to replace after use. This same system is extremely effective with tools and lawn-care equipment.

Here are a few other hanging ideas: hang a pocketed shoe bag to hold things like vacuum attachments. Such bags can also hold cleaning supplies, shoes, socks, curling iron, blow dryer, hair spray, hats, scarves, mittens, sewing items, and any number of things.

Cup hooks screwed onto the bottom rod of a wooden coat hanger can hold many things such as belts, purses, and jewelry. Slip the link of a chain around the neck of a hanger, attach shower curtain hooks every few links, and you've got instant hanging storage for purses, toy bags, or what have you. Sew café rings to the backs of stuffed animals and hang them up and out of the way. Velcro is another alternative.

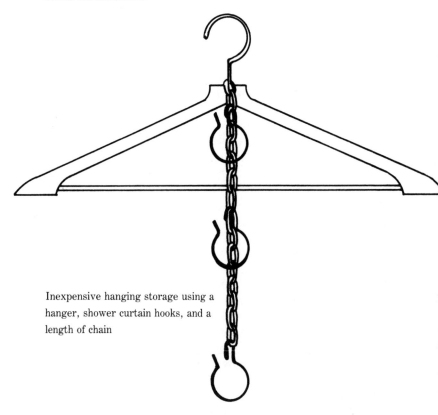

Inexpensive hanging storage using a hanger, shower curtain hooks, and a length of chain

Tension rods provide easy hanging storage. Put one up in the doorway while you're ironing and you've got a convenient, temporary place to hang pressed clothing. Tension rods can also be used to hold wide rolls of wrapping paper. (Or snap the rolls into wall mounted clips of the type used to hang brooms or mops.) A tension rod between two closet walls could be used for additional hanging storage in the closet.

Low closet rods can greatly increase the amount of available closet space. If you don't want to install one, a commercial product is available for about ten dollars. It simply hooks onto the existing rod. For about one to two dollars you can make one yourself.

Cut a one-inch dowel to the desired length. With a screw, attach a piece of chain to both ends of the dowel. Put a shower curtain ring in the last link of both lengths of the chain. Slip the shower curtain hook over the closet rod and snap it shut. You now have a trapeze type closet rod for under two dollars!

A low closet rod using a dowel and
two lengths of chain

A curtain or towel rod can be hung on the back of a door to hold a bedspread or quilt, table linen, your next day's outfit, jewelry, or ties.

Cup hooks screwed to the under side of a shelf or cupboard can hold belts, tote bags, kitchen utensils, tools, jewelry or even cups.

Triple-tiered wire baskets (for fruits and vegetables) can hold whatever you can think of like beauty supplies (such as nail polish, lipstick, shampoo, or soap) or a few small stuffed animals.

As you can see, hanging is one of the most versatile of the four storage alternatives. Use it and see how much space opens up for you.

STORE IT ON THE FLOOR

Here are a few ideas to get you started. When it comes to the floor, don't ignore the space between things. This is especially evident in the kitchen. Do you have a space between the refrigerator and the counter? What about the space between other appliances? These spots are ideal for large trays, cookie sheets, cutting boards, etc. Start inspecting your rooms and notice those small inconspicuous places.

Everyone is familiar with covered under-the-bed boxes that are widely available. An old drawer with casters under each corner can provide ample, rolling storage under a bed. A long dust ruffle under a crib or table hides a large storage area that would otherwise be unused or cluttered looking.

A closet floor may have storage potential. Stacking vegetable bins can hold shoes or folded sweaters. A wastebasket kept on a closet floor can hold hangers. No more pushing clothes back and forth to locate a hanger; and, when washday rolls around, the hangers are ready to take to the utility room.

Large garbage or trash receptacles can hold ski gear in the summer and summer clothes in the winter.

An attractive wicker basket (with a lid) can be lined with a plastic trash basket or plastic bag and used to hold a few extra pounds of sugar, flour, beans, rice or anything, for that matter. A covered wicker basket can also hold dish towels, cleaning cloths, or diapers. These baskets can be placed decoratively in any room.

So if space is a problem, look between and under. The added feature here is that you get more storage space per square foot of floor space. Look on the floor—it's a great storage alternative.

DROP IT INTO A DRAWER

The many uses for drawers are somewhat more obvious than hanging or floors but, if you think creatively, you *can* come up with some novel uses. Anything from paper towels to spices can be stored effectively in a drawer. Jewelry can be kept tangle free in a drawer by storing it in ice-cube trays.

A drawer can give you extra counter space or provide additional table space. Here's how: Open a drawer and place a cookie sheet or cutting board on top. Close the drawer as far as it will go and there's additional work space for you.

Drawers can be hung under existing shelves using U-shaped molding and dishpans. Cardboard shoe files will hold nine shoe boxes that will function like drawers.

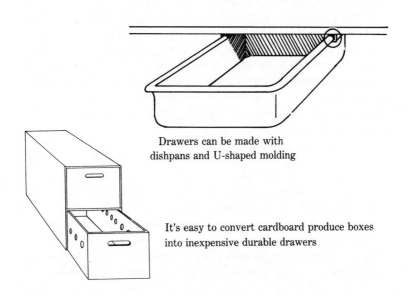

Drawers can be made with
dishpans and U-shaped molding

It's easy to convert cardboard produce boxes
into inexpensive durable drawers

For inexpensive drawers, stack two covered orange or apple boxes. (Ask your grocer to save some of these boxes for you. Some merchants will sell them for a nominal fee. While certain stores recycle them, others toss them out. Call a few grocery stores and see what their policy is.) Cut out one end panel on each of the two lids and cover the sides, top and back with self-adhesive paper. Attach a drawer pull to the front of each drawer and you've got instant and inexpensive drawers.

Virtually anything, providing it's not too large, can go into a drawer. Of all the storage alternatives, though, drawers are the hardest to maintain. Often they become open pits in which to dump anything. A quick shove, the drawer is closed and the unsightly mess is out of view. Drawers almost seem to invite clutter!

DIVIDE AND CONQUER

The answer to functional drawer space is to use plenty of drawer dividers. Inexpensive plastic drawer dividers are widely available at variety stores. Cardboard boxes can be cut to fit the drawer, thus giving everything a specific place.

Drawer dividers can be obtained almost anywhere. They come in a variety of sizes. However, anything that is hollow and rectangular (or square) is a potential divider. Dishpans, ice-cube bins, plastic liners for windowbox planters, cutlery trays, four-sided napkin holders, and cosmetic trays are a few alternatives to regular drawer dividers. Cardboard boxes are free if you're pressed for cash. Throughout the course of this book, you will learn specific ways to use drawer dividers.

I had one particular dresser drawer that was always a mess. It seemed that every week I had to completely redo the whole thing. I was using a few drawer dividers, so I couldn't understand my predicament. After analyzing the situation, I discovered that one drawer divider held three different types of things. Shortly after I separated them, they were once again piled in a jumbled heap.

I removed everything from the drawer and grouped like items together. Next, using small cardboard boxes and plastic shoe boxes, I made individual compartments for each category. Because I was able to cut the cardboard to just the right size, every inch of drawer space was used. The drawer is now extremely functional and stays organized.

As far as drawers are concerned, *divide and conquer* is the rule!

SHELVE IT

There have been whole books written on the subject of shelving; so you can see the popularity and adaptability of this storage alternative. There are a few guidelines, though, that can help make the most efficient use of your shelves.

Shelves, like drawers, can be divided and categorized giving everything a well-defined, well-confined place.

Small items can be categorized and placed in bins, dishpans, buckets, boxes, etc. These organizers can also be used as slide-out trays to make things on a shelf easy to reach.

Shelves that are too deep result in hard-to-use areas, because things need to be stored one in front of the other. Standard twelve-inch shelves will give you one-motion storage and provide a fast, functional system.

Narrow shelves are especially important for high storage because these areas are harder to see and to reach. Wider shelves are okay for low storage as long as you keep high priority things in front to provide one motion storage.

If you're already stuck with deep, awkward shelves, sometimes it helps to put the stored items into a sturdy box that you can slide out. This way everything is easier to see and reach.

Stacked pieces should be placed on lower shelves so they don't topple over when you remove them. A good rule is never to stack more than two high.

Large things (that are not too heavy) that you can remove with one motion are good candidates for storage on higher shelves.

Ideally, shelving should be adjustable to accommodate objects that are varied in size. Adjustable shelves can be mounted on a wall or other vertical surface with track and bracket fittings. Shelves can be suspended with rope or chain from a ceiling.

Shelves need not be expensive. Snap together metal shelves, recycled bookcases, heavy cardboard shelves and particle board shelves (stacked on bricks, cement blocks, or large food cans) are a few less expensive alternatives.

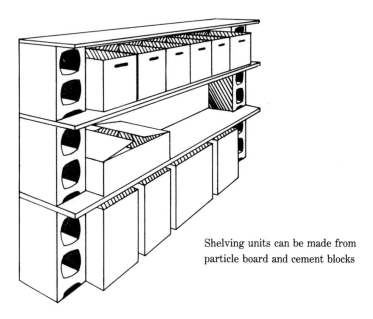

Shelving units can be made from particle board and cement blocks

A small free-standing shelf put inside a closet can be especially beneficial in children's rooms.

Open shelves can add to the cluttered appearance of a home. So, unless you are a naturally neat person, keep your shelves covered with a door, blind, or folding screen.

There you have the four storage alternatives. As you read the many storage ideas in this book, keep the four storage alternatives in mind. They will help you adapt any of the following ideas to the architecture and physical layout of *your* home, dorm, or apartment. Even if you have an efficiency apartment, the four storage alternatives will open up untold areas of unused space.

8

A Kitchen Primer

If you can't find anything but your kitchen sink, then this chapter is for you. My kitchen is the hub of our home, around which our family revolves—so, it's in the kitchen where I make or break my day. Because we spend so much of our time in the kitchen, here's where we can save the most time. Organizing your kitchen and your kitchen time will definitely add extra hours to your day.

Thirty years ago, a study was made of homemakers throughout the country. It was learned that the majority of housewives spent an average of four hours a day in the kitchen! Thank goodness for the wonders of modern technology. Today we have dishwashers, microwaves, food processors, self-cleaning ovens, self-defrosting freezers, and countless other timesaving appliances. Though science has come to our rescue with improved kitchen equipment we can reduce kitchen hours even more by applying organizational principles to our kitchen management.

The average homemaker operates on "kitchen standard time." We make breakfast, clean up breakfast; make lunch, clean up lunch; bake goodies, clean up after baking goodies; make dinner, clean up dinner; make bedtime snacks, clean up bedtime snacks. Get the picture?

After this exhausting ritual, we are often too tired to clean up after dinner or midnight snacks. So we go to bed and start tomorrow doing yesterday's work. Add to this the rigors of a full-time job and the kitchen alone becomes overwhelming (not to mention the rest of the house). It's no wonder we don't enjoy housework!

Let's take the drudgery out of our kitchen work and give it some vision. Using our organizational principles, we can drastically shorten the amount of time we spend in the kitchen.

When it's time to physically organize any area, the first principle to use is *discard and sort*. In the kitchen the application of the discard and sort rules are paramount.

WHAT DOES A KITCHEN MEAN TO YOU?

First, what purpose does your kitchen currently serve? Some kitchens are used only for food preparation and service. Others as family rooms for watching television, reading and doing homework. Some homes have kitchen laundry areas. What purposes do you want your kitchen to serve? After answering this question, you can then decide what essentials need to be handy so the kitchen will function in the desired manner (although you are bound to some degree by the physical layout of the room).

With this in mind, take a look at your kitchen. If you're like most homemakers, your kitchen is full of *things*. Well-meaning salesmen convince us of our need for their products. Manufacturers are constantly coming up with irresistible gadgets. With the best of intentions, friends and relatives are showering us with stuff, too. More than likely, you have an array of unmatched cheese glasses, plastic lids that don't fit anything, whipped topping containers, and margarine tubs. And you have to rummage through a maze of meatball makers, vegetable brushes, egg slicers, cookie cutters, and pancake turners to find your favorite paring knife!

To understand what harm all this junk is doing, remember the three levels of housework: getting ready, doing the job, and cleaning up. Imagine that you're making a cake. To get ready, you have to get the mixing bowl and mixer, the measuring spoons and cups, the rubber spatula, cake pans, and the ingredients. Then you have to grease and flour the pans and preheat the oven.

Think how much longer it takes to make a cake when you have to look for everything. First you move a network of boxes, cans, and jars to find the cake mix. Then you get the mixing bowl. It's not in the cupboard so you rummage through the dishwasher (which was never turned on). So you need to hand wash the bowl before you can use it. The next step is to put the mix into the bowl—no problem. Now, it's time to get the cooking oil that's called for in the directions. Back to the cupboard to retrieve the cooking oil. Add the oil and eggs to the mix. Add to all this the time spent on your hands and knees removing the mixer and its components from the far reaches of the cupboard!

The doing part of cake baking is the actual mixing of the batter and putting it into the oven.

Cleaning up is putting everything away. After touring our kitchen to learn how to better organize his, one man confessed to me his method for cleaning up. When his dishwasher finishes its final cycle, he removes the silverware basket and literally dumps the contents into a convenient kitchen drawer. He swears his system is the fastest he's heard of. "However," he adds, "it takes twenty-five minutes to ferret out six forks to set the dinner table!"

WARS WITH DRAWERS

Do you ever have to rearrange things to get all your paraphernalia to fit back into the cupboards or drawers? Think about that for a minute. Have you ever tried to shut a drawer that was so full you had to nestle everything together so the drawer would close? (The problem here is that sometimes things "un-nestle" and the drawer become impossible to open!) What about the pots and pans? Have you ever gone to put a kettle away and found it necessary to restack the entire set of pans? Have you ever opened a cupboard only to be met by an opened bag of powdered sugar?

Imagine how much time you would save if you could quickly put things back into a specific place, without having to think about it. When your belongings have a well-defined, well-confined place, you can put things away and get ready "automatically."

"Great," you say, "but where do I start?" The first step is to un-clutter. Get down to the basics, the real necessities. Then and only then, can you begin to give things a well-defined place.

UNCLUTTER YOUR DAY— WHEN IN DOUBT, THROW IT OUT!

Since the kitchen is a top priority room, let's get it into shape. Remember our three box system? Now it's time to put it into practice! For this project you need three boxes and a large trash basket. The first box holds anything that belongs in another room. This box keeps you from wandering into other parts of your house and getting sidetracked. The second box holds things to recycle— give away or sell. The third box is for things you're unsure of. It could be called the "ambivalence box." The use for the trash basket is obvious. Use it as often as possible.

Cupboard by cupboard, drawer by drawer, go through everything in your kitchen. As you look at each bowl, each utensil, ask yourself these questions:

1. *Do I need this?* Oftentimes the answer will be "I don't know. I just have it." Is this object performing a useful service to you? If so, then you need it! Or is this article costly in terms of time, clutter, and inconvenience?

Some appliances and gadgets may be more trouble than they are worth. If you never use something because it's time consuming to assemble or requires tedious cleaning, get it out of your kitchen.

2. *How long has it been since I used it?* The answer to this question reveals several things. If you haven't used that platter since Aunt Ethel came for dinner two years ago—out it goes. If something is used often, it deserves one-motion storage in an easy-access location. If it is used occasionally, then it is given two-motion storage or it can be placed in such a way that bending or stretching is necessary to reach it. The frequency of use determines the degree of accessibility.

3. *Do I need so many?* Count the burners on your stove and then count the number of pans you have collected. Maybe you do need all those pans occasionally, but why have all of them in a prime location? Get out all your plastic bowls and put the lids on them. How many extra lids do you have? Get out your cutlery set. How many of those knives do you use all the time? Now, check out your margarine and frosting tubs. I know you use them for leftovers. Many of you use them for homemade frozen preserves, storing individual servings of ice cream, and 1,001 different things. Let's be realistic. How many leftovers do you ever have all at the same time? Why keep adding to the collection? Do you put up frozen jam every week? Then why are these containers piling up in the kitchen until next year? Store them with your other canning supplies.

GET TOUGH

When it comes to question number two, be hard on yourself. Many people have invited me into their homes to give them some ideas on organization. The biggest problem I see is duplication. Most of us feel that if one is good, four is even better.

Sometimes it is wise to have an extra set of measuring spoons and cups, wooden spoons, and other kitchen instruments that are used repeatedly. Some things like casserole dishes and custard cups come in a set. If you're using the whole set, then having these duplicates is fine. On the other hand if some of the casserole dishes are never used, store them out of the kitchen. If you have twelve custard cups and only need six, store the extras out of your way. Don't feel obligated to keep something in your kitchen just because it's part of a set.

It is so easy to rinse something off and use it again. You will also often find that one item can be substituted for another. One reward of this practice is more cupboard and drawer space.

Even though I do a lot of baking, I find that one set of mixing bowls works very well. Why should I clutter my cupboard and waste valuable space by storing three sets of mixing bowls? Really think through your belongings. If you can't part with something, store it in a more inconvenient place and use your handy space for more frequently used things. You can store objects used twice a year, or less, in covered boxes in the basement or garage. The point is to unclutter your kitchen and make your work easier and faster.

A student of mine put this principle to the acid test. Her cupboards were bulging with mixing bowls and she resolved to do something about it. One summer morning she decided to go on a baking spree and bake a three-month's supply of cookies. During the course of two days she baked over one thousand cookies using one set of mixing bowls.

"It was wonderful," she said. "The kitchen stayed so clean. It used to be a mess when I was baking. My counters were always covered with mixing bowls and debris." She had proven to herself that she could manage without all those extra mixing bowls, so out they went. She learned by experience that getting rid of extras forces you to keep your equipment ready for use and in the long run eliminates a lot of extra work!

To review:

- Do I need this?·

- How long has it been since I used it?

- Do I need so many?

These are the golden questions of organization. Once the kitchen is finished, you can use these same principles in every room of your home. By the way, if the answer to any of these questions was: "I'll keep it just in case," or "It might come in handy someday," you are prone to clutter. Get rid of whatever it is.

If you simply can't decide whether or not to discard something, or if you just don't know what to do with it, put it in the ambivalence box, box number three. When the box is full, put it in an inconvenient, out-of-the-way place. Make your possessions earn their place in your home. If you go to the outer limits to dig something out of the box, then that gadget has earned its rightful place. Use it in good health!

As soon as the recycle box, box number two, is full, take it to your favorite charity. Put those things out of your house immediately, and your mind as well.

After spending hours sorting through the kitchen, one woman had a large box of giveaways. Then, she made her first mistake. One afternoon she spread the contents of the box all over her kitchen for her daughters-in-law to choose whatever they wanted. Seeing all those long-forgotten things made her think, "Oh, this might come in handy." Slowly all her hard work was undone.

More than likely, box number one will also be full. This container, remember, holds everything that belongs in another room. These are the things that do not help your kitchen accomplish its desired purpose: the gas bill, a missing sock, the Scrabble game, a half-knitted sweater, etc.

Take the plunge! Enjoy a kitchen that's free from chaos by using the principle of discard and sort.

9

Centering Your Kitchen

Once you've pared down your belongings to a workable few, it's time to start thinking. Think before you act. It helps to look at your kitchen as a series of individual work centers. Generally, there is a mixing center where food is prepared for cooking and serving. There is a sink center where dishes are washed, where you get water for cooking, where vegetables are prepared, etc. You have a cooking center where cooking and baking is done. The refrigeration center is obviously for cold storage of food. We will discuss each center in detail, but first here are some general guidelines that apply.

When replacing kitchen miscellany, think in terms of where something is first used rather than what it is. We have a tendency to put all the food together, all the pans together and all the dishes together, regardless of where we use them. Store things at the point of first use.

For high-priority essentials, provide one-motion storage. This means you can open a cupboard or drawer, reach in and grab it with one motion. You will also be able to replace it with one motion.

Add extra motions depending on the amount of use. For example, the roasting pan or cake platter can be stored on a higher or lower shelf out of your comfortable reach.

As much as possible, keep working surfaces free of decoration, gadgets, and storage. This will simplify any project. Some folks claim they can work under the most adverse circumstances. But, if you're working in a mess you're working in spite of it—*not* because of it.

Ideally, you should store things one layer deep. If this is impossible, store like items behind each other (e.g., one can of tomato soup behind another can of tomato soup, six salad plates behind six salad plates).

Be careful of high storage areas. It is best to keep large, light-weight items high so they can be retrieved with one motion. Using high storage points for stacked or nestled objects can be dangerous. Whenever you find it necessary to stack anything (other than plates), don't stack over two high—three maximum.

DON'T BE DUPED

Learn to think for yourself. This has been a hard lesson for me to learn. I was a real sucker for those gorgeous ads we all see in magazines showing the well-organized kitchen. I spent a lot of money on turntables, round revolving bins, dish organizers, and other little storage "space-savers" only to find that some are very inefficient space wasters. Remember the only way a manufacturer can stay in business is to continually offer new items. We have to decide for *ourselves* as to whether a gadget is necessary and efficient no matter how it's advertised.

The way to give your utensils the well-defined places they need is to use drawer dividers. Many today are fortunate to have built-in dividers, but inexpensive plastic drawer dividers are just as efficient.

My most convenient large drawer is divided into six compartments, one for each of the following groups:

1. Two paring knives, one small serrated knife
2. Can opener and potato peeler
3. Rubber spatula, tongs, wire whisk
4. Two sets of measuring spoons
5. Wooden spoons
6. Two pancake turners

Also in this drawer is my hand mixer, beaters, and two sets of measuring cups that fit nicely in the leftover space. I do have other kitchen utensils that I use. However, I do not use them as often, so they are organized neatly in a different drawer. Having each utensil in its own little space enables me to grab things out of the drawer without even looking!

Having each utensil in a well-defined place gives you easy access, one-motion storage

Use plenty of drawer or space dividers. Cramming causes disorganization. By giving everything well-defined, well-confined places, drawer dividers eliminate cramming.

Dividers can be used in drawers, on shelves (as slide-out trays), and under sinks. Anything that is square or rectangular in shape and hollow is a potential, functional divider. Beware of any round container. They are genuine space wasters.

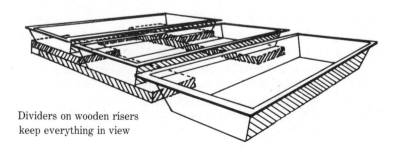

Dividers on wooden risers
keep everything in view

To illustrate the amount of space round containers waste, consider this example. In a freezer, each cubic foot will hold approximately twenty-five pounds in odd-shaped or round containers. On the other hand, if the containers are square or rectangular, each cubic foot will hold forty pounds. (Keep this example in mind every time you're tempted to hang on to just one more whipped topping container!)

One secret of good time management is to develop efficient habits. If you are in the habit of reaching into a specific drawer divider and grabbing your wooden spoon; if you're in the habit of putting the spoon back in the same drawer divider, you are saving time. Multiply this time by the number of things you reach in for and put back and you'll see how those seconds add into minutes. You are reducing the time spent getting ready and cleaning up.

It seems we never have enough storage space even in the largest kitchens. Somehow, everything grows and grows until it fills the space available (and then some). These tips and those that follow will help you get more space and more time!

THE MIXING CENTER

Where should your mixing center be? The ideal place is between the cooking center and the sink, but work around whatever design is available to you.

Time and motion studies have revealed that the most number of trips occur between the stove and the sink. The second largest number of trips is between the mixing center and the sink. It follows that the ideal mixing center is between the cooking center and the sink.

Whenever you whip up a cake, put together a casserole, or make pancakes you work at the mixing center. Here you will need a variety of supplies: staples, mixes, seasonings, measuring equipment, bowls, spoons, and so on. All this equipment will be a major consideration in deciding where to set up your mixing center.

Your goal is to be able to easily reach whatever you need—without taking more than one step or one pivot.

The next time you're performing a routine kitchen task (making coffee, fixing a bowl of cereal, or making a sandwich) notice how you are working. Are several steps necessary to complete the job? If so, a better arrangement of tools and supplies is in order.

The structure of your kitchen may prohibit ideal arrangements. This is often the case, so don't feel discouraged if you're stuck with a kitchen that was designed by someone who never even boiled water. Some kitchens are designed for beauty only and are completely inefficient.

One woman complained to me that her husband (who was a carpenter by trade) built all her kitchen cabinets without one single drawer!

Although, as in my kitchen, a perfect setup is impossible, we can work around any physical imperfections. If after reading this chapter you're still dismayed, go through Chapter Seven, "The Four Storage Alternatives," again. That chapter, in addition to some of the following chapters, will give you some creative solutions to kitchen organization problems.

MIXING IT TOGETHER

What kind of things should be in the mixing center? Anything that helps you prepare food for service. You will need canisters of flour and sugar, baking powder, baking soda, spices, extracts, seasonings, powdered sugar, brown sugar, shortening, whatever you require.

I am not suggesting that all food needs to be placed in this center. Some foods such as dry cereals, crackers, chips, sugar for cereal and coffee, and nondairy creamer do not involve preparation—they go right into the dish. These foods, then, could be stored at a point near the dishes they are served in. This is an example of storing things where they are first used rather than by category.

You will also need such equipment as the mixer, food processor, measuring spoons and cups, stirring spoons, wire whip, spatulas, and anything you deem necessary. We all have our favorite, peculiar little tools.

As with the food, this center does not necessarily have to store all your utensils. The potato peeler, for example, is first used by the sink. The frying pans are first used at the stove as are the wooden spoons. As you can see, if you have your mixing center between the sink and the stove, things will be much less complicated.

The point I am trying to make is that whenever it's practical, store things where they are first used.

Here's how I organize some of my mixing center supplies.

Inside the cupboard door, a set of measuring spoons and cups is hanging for easy reach. Next to this hangs a small clipboard holding my shopping list.

A crock on the counter in my mixing center holds a "bouquet" of necessary equipment (wooden spoons, wire whip, a spatula, etc.). I've always wished for a drawer at my mixing center but that's impossible because of the physical structure of my kitchen. In any case, the bouquet alternative works just as well. Mixing bowls I have stored in a cupboard directly above. The food processor is also in my mixing center, tucked into a corner on the counter.

A bouquet of cooking tools provides one-motion storage in the mixing center

CONTAINED AND CONFINED

Now, here's where the fun begins! (I love to save space.) Think about the things you bring home from the store. You have plastic bags, bottles, boxes and all shapes and sizes of containers. It's hard to store everything neatly when you're dealing with so many different entities and the varying shapes force you to store unlike items behind each other. Sometimes you have to stack just to get everything to fit into the cupboard. One-motion storage seems impossible.

Here's how I solved the problem. The food I use all the time is transferred into square or rectangular plastic freezer containers. These inexpensive little goodies are worth their weight in gold. They come in all sizes and stack easily. The contents of each of the containers is printed on a piece of masking tape with a permanent black marker. Then I put the tape on the side of the container so I can see it readily. When I want to change the contents of the container, the tape can easily be removed.

Because of the uniform shape, everything fits like pieces of a puzzle. I can see all my supplies with one glance, reach in and get what I want with one motion and return it with one motion.

I can find a size of square or rectangular container to suit my every need. Believe me, they come in all sizes. A trip to the discount or variety store will prove it. They come in everything from sizes just big enough for a sandwich, to some that hold two loaves of bread.

Transfer your food into square containers and see how much space you save

I have a separate container for chocolate chips, cornstarch, cake flour, cocoa, oatmeal, Cream of Wheat, powdered sugar, powdered milk, presweetened drink mix, marshmallows, macaroni, cornmeal, etc. I even use these containers for leftovers.

Food stored in these containers stays fresher. The containers also discourage pests, a particularly important consideration in some areas of the country. It is also much easier to measure ingredients. You can dip in a measuring cup or spoon without spilling.

The most striking result will be when you see how much space you've saved. Plus, these labeled plastic containers give all my cupboards the uniform look of organization. Whenever I open a cupboard, it seems to say, "You *are* in control here." What a boost for my self-image.

I use a narrow plastic drawer divider to hold my bottles of extracts, flavoring, and food colorings. I put a small piece of masking tape around the neck of each bottle and label it according to its contents (usually abbreviated i.e., Map X, Al X, Red, etc.). The divider keeps the containers standing in a neat row and I can see at a glance what I want without removing the bottles to read the labels.

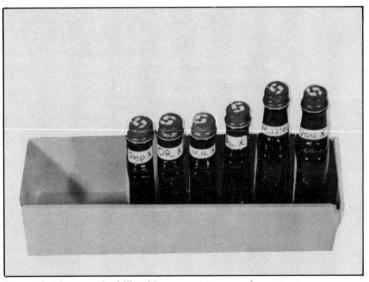

Extract bottles organized like this are easy to use and easy to store

Another plastic divider is used to hold envelopes of drink mixes, whipped topping mixes, seasoning mixes, etc. I stand the envelopes up with the labels facing me. This way, I can flip through them and choose what I want. Again, the drawer divider contains them so they are easy to see, easy to grab and easy to keep organized. A square plastic freezer container could be tacked on the inside of the cupboard door and used for the same purpose.

In a high-priority cupboard where everything is given one-motion storage, there are usually a few inches of shelf space in front of the things you have stored. This space can be put to use by mounting things inside the cupboard door. That way every inch of space is used and you still have one-motion storage.

Flip through your envelope packages like a file and quickly make your selection

I use a plastic bread container (the one-loaf size) without the lid in which I store the plastic lids that always seem to accumulate.

The lids are standing up and are well contained, not piled in a drawer or sliding around the cupboard.

To further simplify this particular storage problem, mark (with permanent marker) the bottom of each plastic container with a symbol, letter, or number. Mark its respective lid with the same symbol, letter, or number. Then when you use a container, you can easily find the right lid.

Herbs and spices can really be a mess to store. Using a permanent black-felt marker, I write the type of spice (usually abbreviated) on the top of the spice can or jar. Then I put the spices in a kitchen drawer in alphabetical order. When I open my spice drawer, all the names of the spices are immediately visible. I can quickly take and replace the spice I need. Putting the spices in alphabetical order makes it much easier to locate a particular spice.

If I were to store the spices in the refrigerator or on a cupboard shelf, I would put them in a plastic drawer divider of whatever size was needed to hold all my spice containers. The divider would also serve as a slide-out tray. My large jars and bottles of spices are on a shelf directly underneath my spice drawer. They, too, are in a plastic drawer divider and all the containers are labeled on the top so I can easily make my selection. Again, I use the divider as a slide-out tray. If you have a drawer large enough to hold all of your spices, so much the better.

Another method would be to use small blocks of wood to build little risers to hold your spices. Or, a clear plastic shoe box placed on a shelf can hold spices. When one is needed, slide out the whole box to make your choice.

Let's explore another center and see how other kitchen areas can be set up efficiently.

THE SINK CENTER

The sink center is the center where you spend the most time. With a little thought, you can use this area to better advantage.

Think before you act. What kind of things are first used by the sink? Generally, vegetables like potatoes, onions, carrots, etc. are handled first at the sink. Those vegetables that do not require refrigeration could be stored in bins near or under the sink. Knives and peelers for preparing these vegetables should be stored near the sink. Condensed soups and other foods that require the addition of water are first used at the sink and can be kept in a nearby cupboard. A can opener should also be handy. Teakettles or a saucepan used to heat water start their use at the sink. Glasses and pitchers also are frequently used first at the sink. Colanders are always used at the sink. Cleaning supplies can be stored under a sink: dish detergent, cleanser, automatic dishwashing detergent, and scouring pads are a few examples. Ideally, the dishwasher should be located close to the sink. Dish storage should be included in this center (whenever practical) to facilitate replacing dishes after they are cleaned.

If you're always in a hurry to get the dishwasher unloaded so you can fill it again, you'll appreciate having your dish storage convenient to the dishwasher.

The sink seems to be the central kitchen area where trash and scraps collect. This would make the sink center an ideal spot for a trash container, compactor or disposal. And with an over-the-sink cutting board, counter space can be expanded and counters kept cleaner.

The sink is such an ordinary thing. There it sits day after day. Did you ever think the day would come when you would organize it? Well, that day has arrived.

DISHWASHERS AND DISHPANS— A DYNAMIC DUO

You might think in this age of dishwashers that the dishpan is all washed up! Not at our house. You'll be hearing a lot about dishpans from me.

In the kitchen I use a dishpan to set and clear the table. I just pile everything into the dishpan, carry it to the table or to the sink if I'm clearing up, and I can make it in one trip. You'll appreciate this idea more if you count the number of times you go back and forth cleaning up after eating. The children really like having the dishpan when it comes time to set the table. I just hand it to them filled with dishes, glasses, and utensils and they get to work. If you have a large family and a dishpan just won't hold everything you need, maybe a heavy plastic kitty litter pan would work.

I use another dishpan as a slide-out tray for cleaning supplies kept under the sink. This keeps things from wandering around and gives me one-motion storage.

If you store your cleaning potions high up out of the children's reach, they'll be awkward for you to reach and handle. But not if you put the dishpan filled with cleaners on the high shelf. Then when you want something, you'll be able to slide out the dishpan with one movement. You can choose what you want and slide it back. No more knocking things over to see what you have or to get what you want. This same method can be used for "keep out of reach" medicines, and your shelves will stay clutter free.

Whoever invented the dishwasher gets my vote for the Nobel Peace Prize! What a boon to kitchen organization!

For some reason, I've always hated to sort and put away silverware. I remember when I was a little girl, my mother would always tell me to eat my peas first so I could enjoy the rest of my dinner. Well, I tried that same principle on my silverware, putting it away first, but it didn't help much. So, now when I put the silverware into the dishwasher, I put the knives in one compartment, the spoons in another, and the forks in another. (When doing this, be sure the utensils don't nestle together and prevent thorough cleaning.) Miscellaneous cooking utensils are placed in the remaining three compartments of the silverware basket.

Since I started organizing the silverware, I feel much better about the job and it really saves time when I'm putting the dishes and silverware away. I'm always hurrying to get the dishes put away because I've got another load of dirty dishes to put in.

I've noticed also that frequently when I'm fixing something, the gadget or dish I need is in the dishwasher. When I always put things into the dishwasher in the same general area, I can reach in fast and grab what I need. (Although dishwasher steam facials are therapeutic, I'm usually in too big a hurry to enjoy them!)

Remember that a dishwasher can wash things other than dishes. Decorative glass from lights and furnace register vents, to name just a few, can easily be tackled and cleaned in the dishwasher.

In the case of the furnace vents, you might want to rinse them in the sink first. If they have been long neglected, they may need a few swipes with a scrub brush. So many times I have cut my knuckles to pieces scrubbing those vents with a tooth brush. Never again. This way, my dishwasher can do all the vents in my house while I do something else.

One word of caution—dishwasher detergents and heat might remove paint from some objects and you must be careful not to put in anything that will break or melt.

What if you don't have a dishwasher? Is there any way to keep from having a kitchen full of dirty dishes? I would keep a dishpan, kitty litter pan, or vinyl wastebasket under my kitchen sink and use it to hold my rinsed, dirty dishes. This would certainly eliminate the untidiness of accumulated dishes and may also prevent you from having to wash dishes so often.

As your troubles go down the drain, let's move from the sink to another kitchen center.

THE REFRIGERATOR CENTER

Open your refrigerator door and take in the view. Do you have jars and bottles scattered here and there? Are there any foreign-looking objects needing attention? How about the crisper, and what is the state of the vegetables therein? Remember, celery is supposed to be firm and crisp. Tomatoes are supposed to be totally red with no black spots or fuzz. If the sight is less than breathtaking, read on.

As I've said, home management experts tell us to have a place for everything and have everything in its place. It's hard to apply this advice to the refrigerator, though. It's such a great catchall; just open the door and start shoving things in. This is why the advice of our home management expert is so important.

First, have a place for everything. It's much easier than it sounds. Designate areas of your refrigerator for certain purposes. For example, the top shelf of our refrigerator holds dairy products and beverages. The second shelf holds anything that needs to be used within a short period of time. This is where all leftovers are put.

On the bottom shelf a plastic bread storage box (without the lid) is a handy slide-out tray holding cheese and lunch meat. Also on the bottom shelf a large square plastic container holds all the bottles and jars that would otherwise find their way into a dark corner. I simply slide out the tray, make my selection and slide the tray back. Give your miscellaneous jars and bottles a well-defined place and watch your organized refrigerator take shape.

Keep your refrigerator organized and its contents handy

Bottles of baby formula can also be stored in a tray or soft drink carton so they can be moved around as a single unit. Difficult things, like watermelon, can be stored easier if a shower cap is placed over the cut end. If you have sandwiches or hamburgers often, place all the sandwich fixings (catsup, mustard, relish, mayo, pickles, luncheon meat, and cheese) in a container and slide out the whole tray with one motion. Set it on the table and you're ready to go.

The storage on the door is convenient for one-motion storage for the condiments that you use all the time. If your refrigerator is several steps from your cooking area, an ice-cube bin holds about three and a half dozen eggs and can be a real step saving container. They can also hold several pounds of margarine and allow you to grab a new square quickly. The same bins make good organizers for the refrigerator freezer. I have one to hold leftover meat and one for leftover vegetables.

Leftovers can cause a real congestion problem. Whenever possible, store them in see-through containers. Leftovers stored in this way will be easier to remember. To save precious space, use square or rectangular containers. And when making your meal plans, don't forget the leftovers. That will also cut down on a refrigerator congestion problem.

WINNING THE COLD WAR

The best way I know to organize the deep freeze is to use heavy cardboard boxes. Use one box for pork and ham, one for roasts, one box for steaks, etc. Of course, freezer baskets are available at a cost, and square bicycle baskets are another possibility.

In a chest-type freezer the boxes (with or without tops) can be stacked, thus using every inch of freezer space to the best possible advantage. When the freezer is full, a map of the freezer can help you locate the needed food quickly. (See illustration on page 88.)

With an upright freezer, simply measure the depth, width, and height of the area between shelves. Then find some heavy cardboard cartons that will fit into the existing spaces and you'll have instant drawers! Cut a small half circle in the front of each box to enable you to pull out the "drawers," and make your selection. Be sure the box fronts are well labeled so you'll know what's inside.

Now, let's go one step further with freezer efficiency. I have a perpetual freezer inventory sheet on a sheet of graph paper hanging inside a kitchen cupboard door. (See illustration on page 89.) On the left side of the sheet I have listed, in alphabetical order, all the things we usually have in our freezer. The vertical columns on the graph paper are numbered along the top and bottom. Then, beside each listed item, I check off the number on hand of that particular food. As I remove something from the freezer, I make an X through the check mark, starting at the right side of the graph paper and working to the left as things are used. I am then able to see how many packages of each category are left.

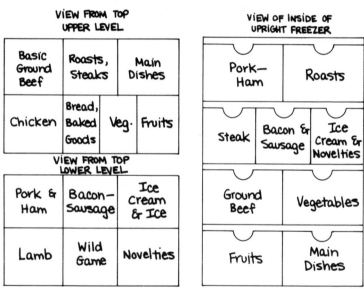

This same type of inventory chart is good for any things you have stored. It can be used for keeping a record of your home-preserved food. It will also give you a better idea of how much food to preserve next year.

I can increase the life of my chart by making the checks and x's in pencil. This way, when food is replaced, I can erase the previous markings and indicate the amount currently on hand. I also reinforce the margins of the chart with transparent tape (the kind you can write on).

				1	2	3	4	5	6	7	8			
BACON				✓	✓	✓	✗							
BASIC G.B.				✓	✓	✓	✓	✓	✓	✓	✗			
BREAD				✓	✓	✗								
CELERY				✓	✓	✓	✓	✗						
CHICKEN				✓	✓	✓	✗							
CORN				✓	✗	✗								
CUBE STEAK				✓	✗									

Now you can open your refrigerator or freezer, stand back and take in the view. Breathtaking, isn't it?

THE COOKING CENTER

At the stove you use pots and pans, lids, griddles, spoons for stirring, hot pads, tongs, and a can opener.

The foods used in this center are things like cooking oil, canned vegetables and other foods you pour directly into the pan, salt, pepper and other seasonings, vegetable coating spray (like Pam, Mazola No-Stick, or Baker's Joy).

Obviously, a cooking center and mixing center right next to each other will prevent you from having to have duplicate items at each (a can opener by the stove and one in the mixing center).

If you have a number of pans, choose four of the most versatile (or the ones you use all of the time) and store them in the cooking center. Put the remaining pans in another cupboard. You won't need them often enough to worry about their accessibility.

It is recommended that pots and pans not be stored in the oven itself. Not only is this practice a fire hazard, it can be hard on your pans if you forget they're inside and turn on the self-cleaning oven!

And the added inconvenience of removing the pans every time you want to bake something makes oven storage a most undesirable practice.

Pans are frequently stored on a cupboard shelf, but a deep drawer might also work if that's all you have available.

I use a plastic bread container (the one-loaf size) without the lid to hold my pot and pan lids. The container slides out from the shelf so I can choose the lid I want. The lids are standing up and are well contained, not piled in a drawer or sliding around the cupboard. Have you ever opened a cupboard and been met by an oncoming frying pan or a barrage of lids? Then you know what I mean. There are also commercial products available especially designed to hold lids for pots and pans. Before buying one, though, make sure all your lids will fit into it.

Make a handy slide-out tray for pot and pan lids
by standing them in a plastic container

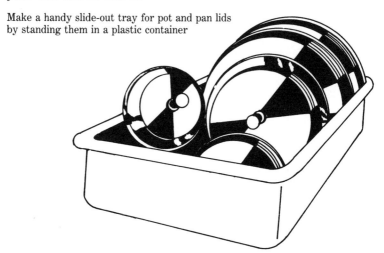

Hanging storage for cooking vessels and utensils is the method used in most restaurants and other commercial kitchens. For home use, though, think about the extra cleaning you'll have to do to keep it all picture perfect. Also, anything hanging near a cooking center is subject to splatters and grease film. With any system you choose, ask yourself it it's worth the time it's going to take to maintain.

Now that we've covered all the centers, use these tips as a guide to help you arrive at the very best arrangement for you. Keep looking for better and faster ways to do things. Notice where things are first used and store them at that point. As solutions unfold, you will wonder why you didn't do this years before! Don't waste any more time. See if a better working arrangement will save wear and tear on you and your kitchen!

10

Taming the Wild Junk Receptacle

Every home has one: the ever-receptive junk drawer. Here lie the half-dead batteries, a few rubber bands, paper clips, the envelope with Aunt Betty's new address, a safety pin or two, copies of credit card purchases, and maybe a piece of gum. There it sits, always willing to accept any little morsel that may come its way.

Where is your junk drawer? Is it in the kitchen, in a night stand or end table? What about the family desk? These are the usual places everyone in the family dumps things they can't classify.

In a sense, this catchall seems convenient; you always know where to find the screw that fell out of the toaster. There is always a pencil inside—if the last user remembered to put it back. This is a great place for all those things you don't want to throw away but don't know what to do with. Yes, the junk drawer seems handy and convenient, but is it really?

Actually, the junk drawer is a menace. It looks awful, and there is no system to it. More than likely, when you really need a junk-drawer item, it won't be there. If, perchance, a needed something *is* in the junk drawer, you will probably have to spend several minutes rummaging.

The key principle when organizing anything from junk drawers to garages is grouping. Everything in a junk drawer can be categorized.

Remove the contents from the drawer and begin: paper clips go into one pile, safety pins into another. Papers necessary for records and needed information should be kept in file folders by subject. (This subject will be covered in detail in Chapter 19.)

Put the buttons with your sewing equipment; the miscellaneous screws where the other screws, nails, and tools are kept. Discard whatever you can. Always store things near the point of first use. Gradually you will bring order out of chaos.

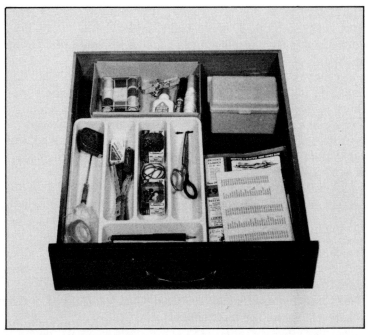

A mini-office center divided into handy groups gives you the ultimate organizer

In our kitchen we have a "mini office center." This is a kitchen drawer close to the phone where we keep many needed supplies. Everything in the drawer is compartmentalized so that each item has a well-defined, well-confined place.

For example, our drawer contains a plastic silverware tray that holds tape, a small stapler, staples, rubber bands, paper clips, thumbtacks, scissors, twist ties for plastic bags, pens, pencils, screwdriver and tape measure.

Next to the tray I have enough room for a small local phone book. Sitting on top of the phone book I keep a 5x8-inch card that has (in alphabetical order) the names and number of the roughly seventy people we call regularly. That card alone has saved me hours of looking up phone numbers in the phone book.

In the back of the same drawer is another drawer divider that holds a little sewing kit for last-minute repairs, a small bottle of glue, my permanent black marker, and a magnetic clothespin for attaching notes to the refrigerator. (The clothespin also makes a great recipe holder.) There is still room left in the drawer for a stack of notepaper (confined in a small freezer container) and my address file.

For names and addresses, I love my 3x5 index card file. Each name and address is on a separate card filed in alphabetical order. There is room on every card to keep any information about the people you want to remember. Birthdays, anniversaries, names of children, gifts given, etc., can all be noted on the cards. And, with this system, deletions and additions are very simple. You'll never have to make up a new address book again.

I use the address file in other ways, too. For example, I can't remember the name of the man we buy tools from, so I have a card labeled *tools*. The man's name, address, and phone number are listed on the card. There's a card for television repair filed under *T*, a card for washer repair filed under *W*. The plumber, whose name escapes me, is filed under *P*. If your memory is better than mine, this system won't be necessary. If not, welcome to the club. (Sometimes I staple business cards right to the file card, rather than recopying all the information.)

This mini office center is not in a large drawer, but it is neatly organized and extremely useful. Locating it by the phone makes it especially convenient. Keeping these supplies in the kitchen is handy because the kitchen always seems to be the center of activity.

If you do not have a drawer available for these useful supplies, you can hang a pocketed shoe bag or other pocketed organizer to keep the things you need within reach. A tool or tackle box is already divided into sections and can be used as a portable office center. A cash box is another alternative. The added feature here is that the boxes can be locked! One family keeps their supplies in a cardboard shoe box. They call it their useful box; and, it *is* useful— they have one on each floor of their home.

We do have a larger office area in our home where office supplies are stored and records are filed. Having the mini office handy and available saves much time and many unnecessary steps.

Above all, remember that this drawer will not stay neat and tidy all by itself. Quietly reinforce your newfound organization by quickly replacing misplaced items. Remove the things that do not belong and put them with their categories. It only takes seconds to maintain, but hours to clean!

Take a deep breath, swallow hard and swear off junk drawers forever.

UTILIZING THE UTILITY CLOSET

I hate to sound relentless, but there may be another junk receptacle in or near your kitchen. If you have a utility closet you have probably noticed that it's used as a dumping ground from time to time.

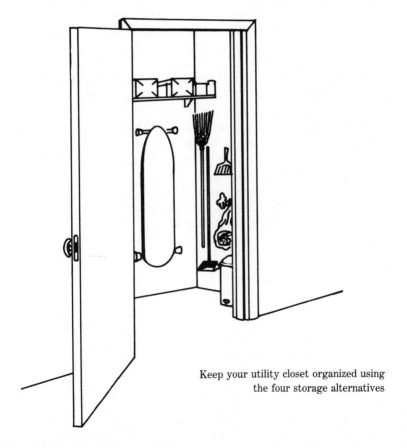

Keep your utility closet organized using
the four storage alternatives

The same principles apply here as applied to the junk drawer. Classify and put away any of the contents that don't belong in the utility closet.

Hang up as many things as you can. Things such as your broom, mop, dustpan, fly swatter, vacuum hose, yardstick, bucket, etc. can all be hung up and out of the way.

If your broom is not equipped with a hook or something you can hang it with, you can always twist a piece of wire around the base of the handle and hang it from there. Drill a hole through the handle or buy the device that snaps onto the end of brooms and mops. Use your imagination. You can usually think of a way to hang (or store) anything.

A pocketed shoe bag can be hung up to hold bottles of cleaners, spray cans, vacuum attachments, or what have you.

If you don't use the vacuum attachments too often, a drawstring bag can be hung and used to hold them. Don't forget to include extra belts, bags, and the instruction booklet.

A pocketed purse file can be hung up to hold large phone books, grocery sacks, plastic wrap, aluminum foil, and whatever you can think of.

Shelf storage is an obvious alternative that can also be used to keep the closet neatly organized. When storing several objects on a shelf, remember to confine them in a shallow box or dishpan so they can be handled as one unit.

No matter what shape your closet is in now, you can discard, sort, and classify its contents. Then, using some creative storage alternatives, you can work wonders!

11

Curing Mealtime Madness

Every day, throughout the world, our voices rise in unison: "What am I going to fix for dinner?" That plaintive cry, coming at about 4:30 in the afternoon, has caused more panic than the stock market crash on Wall Street in 1929. With mealtime minutes away, dread and terror strike. We scramble here and there scrounging up a miscellany of foods to throw on the table.

No matter what my day has been like, the atmosphere at mealtime is not usually conducive to leisurely poring through my Julia Child cookbook. While it's not easy to serve a well-balanced, nutritious meal without slaving away in a hot kitchen, there are a few strategies that help me cope with hectic dinner hours.

Let's begin with the first basic organizing principle: think before you act. Applied specifically to meals, this principle means planning menus!

Every meal you serve should fulfill four goals:

1. The meal should be nutritious.
2. The meal should fit into an established food budget.
3. The meal should please the family.
4. The meal should fit your time and energy limits.

Careful meal planning can reduce mealtime madness and assures the realization of these four basic goals.

GOAL NUMBER ONE: GOOD NUTRITION

Volumes have been written on the subject of nutrition. It is the theme of countless newspaper and magazine articles. As science unfolds the mysteries of various diseases and ailments, we have become progressively aware of the importance of nutrition. I am not qualified, nor would space permit me, to adequately cover the subject, but I can say for a fact that planning menus will improve the nutritional values of your meals.

PEAS AND CARROTS FOREVER

Here's how. When meals are left to chance and we throw together whatever we can find, we're usually thinking only of goal nunber three (the meal should please the family). My general thinking on days like this is, "Right now I've just got to get everyone fed and satisfied. I'll serve peas and carrots tomorrow!" (I *always* promise to do better tomorrow!) Planning helps me focus on the other goals as well.

When meal plans are recorded, you can almost see what you're going to serve, so bad combinations are easier to detect. For example, if your meal plans are only in your mind you may not realize that you are about to serve a pineapple fruit cup, a Jell-O fruit salad, and strawberry pie at the same meal. On paper the mistake is obvious.

You may also notice that you've duplicated ingredients in a casserole and salad—macaroni salad served with pasta, for example.

You will have an overview of how the food is being prepared. For example, fried potatoes, fried chicken and fried eggplant indicates that all courses are fried. From a nutritional standpoint we don't need to eat so many fried foods. Also, preparing everything in the same fashion eliminates the variety needed for palatable meals. A menu including creamed potatoes, harvard beets, and cottage pudding gives you a meal with too many sauces. Sometimes you'll "see" too much of one color. It's easier to visualize your meal when your plans are written.

From the first grade we've been taught about the four basic food groups: the meat group; the milk group; the fruit and vegetable group; and the whole grain, enriched, or restored cereals group.

Today more than ever before we have a wealth of nutritional information at our fingertips. Putting this knowledge to use we can lead stronger, healthier, and longer lives. It's enough to make Richard Simmons proud!

GOAL NUMBER TWO: MEALS WITHIN THE BUDGET

There are a number of ways in which meal planning will help you stay within a given food budget. If your family sits down to a real groaning board on Monday night, you can compensate with less expensive meals on Tuesday and Thursday. You have control over the menu and the cost of the meal because of planning.

Having your meal ideas recorded lets you shop from a specific list, lessening the number of impulse purchases (which, by the way, is a major reason for overspending). With firm plans in mind you can take advantage of coupons, advertised and in-season specials.

Left-to-chance meals require extra trips to the market to fill in missing ingredients. Staying out of stores is one of the best methods for saving money because every visit tempts us to buy extras that unnecessarily eat up the food budget.

Frantic thrown-together meals often include costly convenience foods. Scheduled meal plans help you manage your food preparation time better so convenience foods are not necessary.

Meal plans can also help you include leftovers and cut down on waste.

Mealtime madness drives many of us to fast-food restaurants. While these occasional treats are a nice, but costly, diversion, meal planning will cut our dependence on these facilities.

GOAL NUMBER THREE: MEALS THAT PLEASE THE FAMILY

If there were no other goal but this, the meal manager would have an easy job. But combined with the other goals this becomes increasingly difficult to achieve. Add to that the likes and dislikes within any given family and you have what seems to be insurmountable odds. Sometimes it's a real coup to have meals eaten without complaint and with real enjoyment! Once again, meal planning can help.

If you were to ask a thousand people, "What makes a meal pleasing?" you would get hundreds of different answers. But the responses would probably fall into three main areas:

1. It has to please the senses (looks good, smells good, tastes good).
2. It must satisfy hunger.
3. It should offer variety, not only within the meal itself, but from meal to meal.

Of these three areas, variety is by far the most important consideration. If a wide assortment of foods are offered, the senses will be pleased and hunger will be satisfied.

For me, there is nothing more frustrating than to finish a meal and, thirty minutes later, find one of the kids in the kitchen looking for a snack. Satisfying hunger, then, is an important consideration for me.

If someone walks in the front door, sniffs, and says, "Lasagne again?" you've probably fallen into a monotonous meal routine. If your meals have become banal and boring, menu planning can give you a change of pace.

Ethel Kennedy, wife of the late Senator Robert Kennedy (and mother of eleven), used a two-week rotating menu plan. In this way she was assured that a meal was never repeated more than once every fourteen days.

Whatever method you use, menu planning will help you remember that you served fried chicken Monday night and maybe Thursday is too soon to have baked chicken on rice. Saving your menu plans from week to week will help you see if something is being repeated too often to provide a good variety. Also, you may be reminded of favorites that haven't been served for a while.

Menu planning is especially valuable to those on restricted diets. When foods are limited, it's easy to begin serving the same things over and over again. A written plan will help you stay creative.

Particularly in a family with children, it is hard to please everyone at every meal, but menu planning can contribute to a delicate balance by helping you add variety. When a wide assortment of foods are available everyone can find at least a few things they can enjoy and fill up on.

GOAL NUMBER FOUR: MEALS WITHIN TIME/ENERGY LIMITS

If you were to ask me, "Why do you plan menus?" my immediate answer would be, "Because it saves so much time!" As important and necessary as the other goals are, saving time is my number one reason for menu planning.

When meals are planned with regard for your day's activities you can set realistic time and energy limits. With four boys, we are frequently down at the Little League field from 5 p.m. until 9 p.m. On those days I serve tacos or sloppy joes—not beef stroganoff with wild rice. As much as possible, let your calendar or appointment book guide your menu selection so your meal plans can fit into available time limits. Ask yourself, "How much time am I willing or able to spend?" There's no reason to plan if the plans cannot be carried out.

Menu planning will save you time because you know in advance what you are fixing and you can eliminate extra or eleventh-hour trips to the store. Since all your supplies and ingredients will be ready to use, your plans will run smoothly, avoiding last-minute changes. How many times have you changed meal plans at the last minute because you didn't have (and couldn't borrow) a missing ingredient?

Planning ahead allows you to fix food in advance and dovetail food preparations. Here is where you shave hours off kitchen time. (These accrued benefits will be given major consideration later in the book.)

So, think before you act. Meal planning will help you reach the goals for a successful meal. But more than that, it will still that harping voice on your mind's far periphery, "What am I going to fix for dinner?"

A SMORGASBORD OF MENU PLANNING IDEAS

"Be a good cook," Mother used to say, "and you'll get a man!" What Mother forgot to mention was that you'd also be responsible for planning, preparing, and serving about fifty thousand meals throughout the course of your lifetime. (Thanks, Mom!)

Well, times have changed and we've all come a long way since Mother uttered those famous words. No longer is the kitchen a sanctuary for lovelorn maidens. Men and women alike are beginning to share the fifty thousand meals' responsibility.

In any event, if you're the meal manager, you could probably use some menu planning ideas to get you going.

Before you begin, you will need to gather a few supplies: paper, pencil, and your favorite recipes. As soon as you're ready, begin making a list of all the main dishes you serve for dinner. Group chicken and poultry dishes on one page, ground beef meals on another, etc. The categories I use are: Beef, ground beef, poultry, fish, pork, and miscellaneous. Use the categories that make it easiest and most convenient for you. If you're extremely ambitious, you can do the same thing with side dishes such as potatoes, rice, and vegetables. If you fix dessert every night, you may want to list them too.

As you list the name of each dish, list all the ingredients needed to make that particular main course. This is not a recipe, just a simple ingredients list. Although, when more than one package or can is needed, I indicate it.

SAMPLE MENU SELECTION SHEET

CHICKEN

- *Fried Chicken*   Chicken, oil, flour, salt, pepper
- *Chicken & Rice*   Cooked chicken, cream of mushroom soup (2 cans), milk, cooked rice

- *Chicken-Broccoli*   Cooked chicken, broccoli (2 pkgs.), cream of chicken soup (2 cans), mayonnaise, lemon juice, cheese, bread crumbs
- *Chicken Noodles*   Chicken, onion, celery, flour, milk, salt, bouillon
- *Chicken Rolls*   Cream cheese (2 small, 1 with chives), margarine, pepper, chicken, chicken broth, corn starch, crescent rolls, crumbs, chopped walnuts, sage

Right now, you're probably rolling your eyes and thinking, "Sure, when am I going to do all this? I don't even have time to fix dinner!" Don't think of this as a one-shot project. Break it down into little pieces. You can work on the *chicken* page this afternoon and start *fish* tomorrow evening. You can do a little during your coffee or lunch break. I know one meal manager who worked on it while traveling. Break the job down and use snatches of time that would otherwise have been squandered.

This may take several pages, depending on your repertoire. But, when you're finished, you'll be in the driver's seat instead of under the rear wheels.

These menu selection sheets serve many timesaving purposes. When you're making up menus, you will have all the possibilities right in front of you. There's no need to remember what your family likes because the menu selection sheets have it all recorded.

Menu selection sheets lift the burden of menu planning. Using them, you can choose one or two items from each page for a week or two of versatile, stimulating meals.

When making your shopping list, you have all the ingredient information at your fingertips. No need to check cookbooks or recipe cards to see if you need cream of mushroom or cream of chicken soup, or try to remember if this recipe uses sour cream. And when you're stuck with leftovers, the menu selection sheets can help you choose a good way to use them!

The menu selection sheets serve many other useful purposes. If you like to have surplus food storage on hand, the menu selection sheets can remind you of the things you'll need to have in reserve.

I keep my sheets in my planning notebook. This way if I'm in a store and see a special on round steak, I can easily choose a good way to use it. Also, any extra ingredients that I'll need will not be forgotten. When I find myself waiting at the school or doctor's office, I can plan my menus because my menu selection sheets are always handy.

Imagine the fun you'll have running through the grocery ads. When you notice a great can't-pass-it-up buy, the menu selection sheets will show you all the possibilities for their use.

Included with your menu selection sheets (in your planning notebook) you can make notes from January to December listing seasonal fruits and produce. Then, you will be able to plan effectively for their use.

Save time, save money, and save your family from monotonous meals with the menu selection sheets. Don't leave home without them!

CHOOSE A MENU PLANNING SYSTEM

Once you've completed the menu selection sheets, pick the method that's best suited to your meal planning needs:

1. Get a monthly calendar, the type with large squares. Now, referring to the menu selection sheets, write down in each square what you want to fix for dinner every evening during the month. Be sure to leave a few blanks for leftovers and new recipes to try. If you can't do a whole month, plan a week or two.

I don't especially like to plan menus, so I try to get it over with in one sitting. If, however, you enjoy the activity, you will likely want to do it once a week or so, depending on your time and energy limits. Also, take into consideration how often you want to shop. If you only shop once every two weeks, then menus will have to be planned two weeks in advance.

When it's time to shop, check your menu plans and the ingredients list. Prepare your shopping list by writing down the ingredients you need to prepare your scheduled meals. Just be sure to purchase enough planned ingredients to last from one shopping trip to the next.

Again, having this ingredient list handy is so much easier than going to your cookbook or recipe file to see what you need for every dish.

2. Make up a two-month schedule and rotate all year long. This way, you'll only make menus once in a lifetime! Leave some blank spaces for leftovers and new recipes to try. They can easily be added to your menu selection sheets if they become favorites. With this plan, all you'll have to do is to check your ingredients list and make your shopping list.

3. Plan seasonal menus. Try a "plan for all seasons"—a rotating schedule for fall and spring, schedules for winter meals and summer meals. For some reason, chili, stew, and roast turkey taste better on cold winter nights. Grilled meat and fish, fresh fruits and vegetables seem more satisfying in the summer. The "plan for all seasons" can be used to remind you when a supply of a particular food is abundant. Things like strawberries, peaches, sweet corn, and garden fresh tomatoes have a short season. By using a plan, you can take full advantage of the harvest. As with all the other menu planning methods the "plan for all seasons" will also allow you to have chicken every Sunday, if that is a family tradition.

4. Rather than assign a certain meal to a specific day, just make a list of ten to fifteen meals. (The number of meals you plan depends on how often you shop.) Within this list schedule some quick dishes and some that require a little more time. Next, stock up on all the ingredients needed to make these dishes. Then, when you see what the day is going to bring, simply choose one of the meals on your list, picking the one that will best fit the family's circumstances. Your choice may be determined by any of the following factors:

How much help will be available for dinner preparation?
How many people will be home to eat the meal?
How much time will you have to prepare and serve the meal before people scatter?

As you can see, this is a good plan for those who have several conflicting schedules within the family—especially when no one lets you in on the plans until the last minute.

Using any of the meal planning methods, you can incorporate a few other ideas.

Check grocery ads, in-season specials, and coupons. Refer to your menu selection sheets and see how you can best use good buys. Referring to the ingredient list, jot down the ingredients necessary to complement your meals.

Ask each family member what he or she would like to have one night during the week (or month). Be sure to round out their ideas to provide adequate nutrition. This menu idea works best when used with one of the four preceding suggestions.

All of these systems allow for new recipes, and you can repeat the family favorites as often as you like.

After your menus are planned, go to your deep freeze and bring up all the items you will need for a week. Store these foods in your refrigerator freezer. So many times our dinner plans go awry simply because we don't get the meat defrosted. If your frozen ingredients are handy you'll be more likely to get them thawed and ready. Besides, why make seven trips to the freezer when you need only make one?

If you have a separate food storage area or pantry, bring all the weekly ingredients to your kitchen mixing center and have them handy, too. How many times have you sent somone running to get a can of soup or a box of macaroni? Besides, it's nice to have everything within reach when you're busy fixing dinner.

Remember the time chart for ironing a shirt? The same principle applies here. You can save a lot of time getting ready if you bring everything to the kitchen at once rather than running back and forth every time you're ready to fix a meal.

Keep your menu plans in the kitchen so you can remind yourself first thing in the morning what you have planned. Just knowing what you're going to fix for dinner that night can really lighten your load. You'll also be able to fix what you can after breakfast and thus eliminate some preparation and cleanup at dinner time.

Remember that getting ready and cleaning up are the two areas where most time is wasted. My best managed days occur when I bake after breakfast and prepare ahead what I can for lunch and dinner. I have eliminated much of the get-ready and clean-up for those remaining meals.

12

Are You Filing or Piling Recipes?

Chances are somewhere in your house there is a box, drawer, or basket stuffed with recipes you're going to try someday. These are the recipes that are going to make you the best cook on the block, right?

Maybe that new brownie recipe you saw is better than the one you're using now. Afterall, we can't make second-rate brownies, can we? They have to be the *best*. There's a little "one-upmanship" in all of us when it comes to cooking.

Searching for and saving new recipes is a wonderful boon to menu planning and good eating only if the recipes are used. Why wait for that great and glorious day when you will spend hours digging through your collection trying to ferret out something new to try?

A good recipe filing system allows you to clip and save to your heart's content. It also makes the recipes easy to find, which makes them more usable.

Here's the method I use. Maybe it will work for you, too. I purchased 3x5-inch recipe divider cards with headings such as *appetizers, beverages, cookies, meat, and main dishes*. There were a few categories that I changed for our particular purposes. For example, I have a lot of bar cookie recipes, so I made a divider for bar cookies. I also like having a section for canning and freezing. I put the dividers into a recipe file box. Behind each category our tried-and-true recipes are filed in alphabetical order. Remember, this card file is only for the recipes we have tried and enjoyed. I don't clutter it up with recipes I will never use.

The card file can lead you to the page of a cookbook, too. For example, if you don't want to copy down the recipe for swiss steak, make out a recipe card that says *swiss steak*. Underneath the heading write the name of the book where the recipe can be found, such as: *Hearty Main Dishes*, page 28. This helps if you have a lot of cookbooks and can't remember which book a particular recipe is in.

Next I got several letter-sized file folders and gave them these headings: *appetizers, beverages, breads, breakfast, cakes, frostings/fillings, candy, canning and freezing, cookies, desserts* (miscellaneous) *diets, holidays, main dishes* (meat, fish, etc.), *pies, vegetables,* and *salads.* The folders fit nicely into a large shoe box.

When I see a recipe I'd like to try, I tear it out (when possible) or photocopy it and file it in the proper file folder. Then, when the recipe is tried and enjoyed, I file it in the card file. (Whenever I can, I staple or glue the original recipe onto the file card. Otherwise, I hand copy it or type it on the file card.) If we didn't like the recipe, I just toss it away.

Frequently, you'll find recipes for a meat dish, beverage, and dessert all on the same page. What then? Spend the few seconds it will take to cut the recipes apart. It only takes a moment to do this and it will increase the likelihood that you'll use the recipe.

If you are a cookbook collector, try to keep handy only the cookbooks you use all the time. I have my basic cookbooks in the kitchen. The others are on the bookshelves with the other books. I can easily get to them and use them, but they aren't wasting valuable kitchen space.

So, if you're still collecting one delicious-sounding recipe after another (and you already have 659 untried recipes piled up somewhere) tell yourself that you are *saving*—not cooking. You're becoming a better recipe clipper, not a better cook. Don't waste time clipping—start filing and cooking!

SHOPPING SHORTCUTS

Hanging inside a kitchen cupboard door I have a small clipboard with a pad and pencil. On this pad I write the grocery list I have compiled from my menu selection sheets. Also, when I run out of a certain item, I simply open my cupboard door, grab the pencil and jot it down. It is also easy for other family members to use and contribute to. This way I always have a grocery list on hand and I won't forget a needed item.

When I'm ready to go shopping, all I have to do is grab my clipboard and go. At the store, the clipboard stands in the child's seat of the grocery cart, or it can be held by a child. This way, the list is easily visible, and I can cross out items as I take them from the shelves. Coupons I am going to use are also clipped to the board. The clip can secure bottle deposit receipts or trading stamps.

Make the most of the time you spend shopping. We've already discussed how meal planning can eliminate unnecessary and frequent trips to the store, but here are a few other techniques that will help conserve time.

1. Limit shopping trips, as much as possible, by keeping reserve supplies on hand. If you have plenty of storage space and keep it stocked, you will be able to reduce the number of shopping excursions. This need not be expensive. Coupons, refunds, and special case lot sales can reduce your costs considerably.

2. Shopping from an organized list can speed you through supermarket aisles. Print up a form for your grocery list. Some categories to include might be: *dairy, canned goods, produce, meat, frozen foods, bakery, spices and condiments, household* (cleaners, gadgets, detergents, etc.) *health and beauty aids, pet supplies* and *miscellaneous nonfood*. When you have your form completed, photocopy several to have on hand. As you run out of a needed commodity jot it down on the printed form placing it in its respective category. When you're shopping you will have everything grouped and will eliminate time spent backtracking.

Some experts suggest making a list organized according to the way your favorite market is arranged. This format is not as versatile because it functions well only in that particular store. Also, when stocks of merchandise are rearranged, your printed list becomes obsolete.

3. Shop at a time of day and on a day of the week when congestion is at a minimum. Call the store manager and ask when the best time is. Also check to see if the advertised specials will still be available at that time. Ask if there will be adequate stock to choose from and about the availability and freshness of produce and bakery products. There's no point shopping during low-traffic hours if you can't complete your entire list.

4. Get into the habit of replacing things before the supply is exhausted. As soon as you notice something is running low, add it to your list.

5. Whenever possible, pack your own groceries. That way, things that belong in certain areas of your house can be grouped together and will take much less time to put away.

With rising prices and tight time schedules, I've come to regard shopping as a necessary evil. Even though it may never be a heavenly experience, I try to make it less painful saving all the time I can!

13

Accrued Benefits in the Kitchen

Whether you're busy going to and from work or to and from violin lessons, you'll be happy to discover even more ways to provide your family with a nutritious, tasty, and quick meal. By using the principle of accrued benefits, you honestly can save time without sacrificing quality.

Accrued benefits really pay off in the kitchen! Chances are, you know all about this principle but how often do you put it into action? Whenever possible, get two for the price of one.

For example, how many times have you doubled a recipe, one to serve and one to freeze? That's an accrued benefit. You get the immediate reward (the dinner you serve) and an accumulated reward (the dinner you serve at a later date). You've had one get ready, one cleanup, and two benefits. That's two for the price of one.

Whenever possible, cook with more than one meal in mind. This will not only save precious time, but money as well. Buying larger cuts of meat or buying in quantity is frequently less expensive.

At the risk of sounding redundant, planning ahead is a surefire method that always pays big time dividends. Use kitchen time to prepare as much as possible. For example, start tonight's dinner this morning: prepare a gelatin salad or dessert, chop vegetables for a stirfry meal, marinate the meat. You can even make extra juice for tomorrow's breakfast and prepare sandwich fillings for lunch.

All we're doing is combining the cleanup of one job with the get ready of another. With careful planning, there's no limit to possibilities.

Benefits can grow even larger with careful menu planning. For example, if you plan chicken chop suey for Monday night, prepare extra rice for Wednesday's filled beef roll. That's two for the price of one.

When planning your menus, try to include as many leftovers as possible. After the principle of accrued benefits becomes a working force in your life, leftovers will be better called "planned-overs"!

At this point, however, leftovers may be causing a few problems. Many of us put leftovers back into the refrigerator with the best of intentions. "This time I'm going to remember what's in here and use it." Days and days go by and the leftover collection expands. Pretty soon the refrigerator is so full that we are forced to clean it out. With fear and trembling we open containers wondering what colors and odors await discovery. Most of our "good intentions" are tossed down the garbage disposal. Sound familiar?

There are a few things you can do to help in your battle against mold and fuzz. First, designate a certain area of your refrigerator where leftovers will be kept. Keep the leftovers in this assigned spot. In our refrigerator the second shelf is for leftovers and other food that needs to be used within a short period of time.

Second, putting leftovers in clear containers makes it easier for you to see what's inside, thus reminding you to use the contents.

Third, have a convenient place where you can quickly jot down leftover food, putting the date next to each item. A good place for such a list is inside the cupboard door where most of your food is kept. Hang a small pad and pencil out of sight and you have a quick, efficient place to keep track of your leftovers. (Or attach a magnetic clip to the refrigerator door.) Whenever you're preparing a meal, check your list to see if any of the leftovers can be incorporated into your meal plans. Cross off anything you use. It will take a few extra seconds to write down an item on this list, but it will eliminate much waste and over a period of time it will save you a lot of money. Another benefit is that it keeps your mind on leftovers. Sooner or later, by being reminded of them, you will discover creative ways to use leftovers or to eliminate them.

When planning your menus, try to include as many leftovers as possible. You can even *plan* leftovers (prepare extra mixed vegetables for Sunday's fried chicken and use the leftovers in Tuesday's beef stew).

Check your favorite cookbooks for new ideas using leftovers. In the meantime, here are a few suggestions.

- Vegetables and meats are used well in soups and stews.

Leftover roast or ham can be ground and mixed with other ingredients to make a tasty sandwich spread.

- Leftover waffles? Wrap individually and freeze. When needed, pop into the toaster.

- Chicken or turkey can be used in chicken salad or macaroni salad. An array of easy-to-fix poultry casseroles fill the pages of any cookbook. Poultry can also be made into a delicious spread for canapes and other hors d'oeuvres.

- Leftover ham is ideal in chef's salad or in a scalloped potatoes casserole. There's always ham-potato salad and ham-macaroni salad.

- Pork has may uses in oriental dishes and is especially good heated in barbecue sauce, served on a bun.

- Shrimp, tuna, or salmon are used well in salads and sandwich fillings. Creamed tuna or salmon can be the beginning of a flavorful, nutritious meal.

- Beef, lamb, or veal can also be served in a variety of casseroles; or, simply heat sliced meat in gravy and serve with potatoes, rice or bread. Don't forget the possibility of homemade meat pies.

In addition to their use in soups and stews, vegetables can be attractive and nutritious complements to salads and potato-egg dishes.

Why, you can even make watermelon pickles from the leftover watermelon rind. Leftover pickle juice can be used to marinate raw vegetables. With a simple, effective solution to help you keep track of your leftovers and the unlimited possibilities for their use, there's really no reason to waste anything; especially your time!

Try the principle of accrued benefits. At first it may take some deliberate thought, but the time rewards are so satisfying that accrued benefits will soon become second nature!

14

Meal Management

"I haven't even started dinner and my dish towel is already at half mast!" Do you ever feel like that? If so, don't despair. It's time for a crash course in meal management. Here we go!

MEAL MANAGEMENT 101

What is management? For some people it's when they *manage* to get through the day! Actually, efficient management is achieving maximum output with a minimum amount of time and energy. Sounds too good to be true, doesn't it? With good meal management skills, though, it is easily possible.

Here are a few guidelines that will aid you in your pursuit of your meal management degree.

1. Do similar jobs (such as preparing vegetables) consecutively one after the other. Try to work in one area, doing tasks, simultaneously in the same work center whenever possible. For example, several things can be cooking or baking at the same time.

Remember to work in one area as much as possible. If you followed the basic guidelines for setting up a mixing center in the kitchen, things will be greatly simplified. When you stay in one spot you only need to clean up one spot!

2. Whenever possible, try to complete one task before beginning another. (Prepare *all* the vegetables; finish the table setting before carving the roast.) Using a time chart (as explained later) will help you establish logical priorities in your meal preparations.

3. Remember that you will probably be interrupted. Make sure your time schedule will allow for the unexpected. If you could feasibly prepare your planned meal in sixty minutes, allow yourself

seventy-five. This will work in a little extra time for unexpected phone calls, accidental spills, and directing family traffic.

4. (This is the most important point to remember!) Clean up as you go—by washing (or rinsing), drying, and putting away the equipment you've used. At least 50 percent of the time we spend cooking is spent waiting. Use this time to clean up as you go! Whether you're fixing a batch of cookies or preparing a seven-course meal, start by having a sink full of hot, sudsy water. Also have a trash bag nearby. This will speed up those spot cleanups.

Imagine yourself sitting down to enjoy a nutritious meal with no visible signs of preparation gracing the countertops or piled in an unsightly mess in the sink. If atmosphere is important in a restaurant, it is equally important at home.

Eating is more relaxed and gratifying when you're not surrounded by chaos. It's easier to face after-meal cleanup when the situation is under control. When things don't look too bad, recruits are easier to round up, too.

Return supplies immediately. Remember that it is better to use the same equipment over and over rather than using *more* equipment. The more you have, the more you have to take care of.

5. Set the table completely during free waiting time. Fill the glasses and put other necessary accessories on the table. Set out serving pieces. The last few minutes before a meal is served are difficult because there are so many last-minute details demanding your attention. So, have the table taken care of and out of your way. To simplify setting (and clearing) the table, use a dishpan, tray, or wheeled cart so everything can be carried in one trip.

6. Delegate as much as you can without causing kitchen congestion. Too many people in the kitchen is almost as bad as having to do the whole thing alone!

7. When more than one dish requires last-minute attention, prepare first the one that keeps the best. For example, mash the potatoes before you make the gravy.

MANAGING THE BIG MEAL

Once you have mastered the practices listed above, you're ready to tackle a big, important meal. As with any job, using the right tools is important to insure success. All you need are: paper, pencil, recipes and the clock!

Whenever I have a large "company's coming" dinner to prepare, I use these tools to make a time chart. It's foolproof—success is guaranteed!

As an example, let's go through the steps necessary to manage a Thanksgiving dinner. Consider the following menu:

Roast turkey with stuffing, mashed potatoes with giblet gravy, sweet potatoes, cranberry sauce, green bean casserole, relish tray, blueberry salad, homemade rolls, pumpkin pie.

Referring to your menu, make a list of all the little nonfood jobs that will be required: Set table; fill glasses; set out dessert dishes and serving pieces and miscellaneous table accessories; bring up extra chairs from basement; press table linens and napkins; order centerpiece.

The next step is to decide what you can prepare the day before the big meal. To make day ahead: blueberry salad, pie, cranberry sauce, turkey broth with giblets for gravy and stuffing.

On the left-hand side of a piece of ruled paper, list the menu. Then, make three vertical columns to the right. Label the columns *prepare; cook and ready to serve*; and *total*, respectively. In the appropriate column, list how much time it will take to prepare the item for cooking and how much time it takes to cook and/or get it ready to serve (e.g., assemble and bake the casserole, bake and carve the meat). The two time figures are totaled in the *total* column.

MENU	PREPARE	COOK/ READY TO SERVE	TOTAL
Roast Turkey	15 mins.	5 hours	5 hours 15 min.
Giblet Stuffing	20 mins.	Cooks with turkey	20 mins.
Relish Tray	20 mins.	5 mins.	25 mins.
Mashed Potatoes	10 mins.	35 mins.	45 mins.
Giblet Gravy	5 mins.	10 mins.	15 mins.
Rolls	3 hours 30 mins.	30 mins.	4 hours
Sweet Potatoes	5 mins.	30 mins.	35 mins.

Green Bean Casserole	5 mins.	30 mins.	35 mins.
Pie	Day Ahead	5 mins.	5 mins.
Salad	Day Ahead	5 mins.	5 mins.
Cranberry Sauce	Day Ahead	5 mins.	5 mins.

After your chart is completed, list all menu entries in decreasing order of total time. Here is what the sample menu would look like:

Roast Turkey	5 hours 15 minutes
Rolls	4 hours
Mashed Potatoes	45 minutes
Sweet Potatoes	35 minutes
Green Bean Casserole	35 minutes
Relish Tray	25 minutes
Giblet Stuffing	20 minutes
Giblet Gravy	15 minutes
Pie	5 minutes
Salad	5 minutes
Cranberry Sauce	5 minutes

For illustration, let's plan to serve dinner at two o'clock. It is possible that this dinner could be prepared in 5 hours and fifteen minutes—the time required for the turkey. However, to make room for interruptions and to provide a more leisurely atmosphere, let's allow six hours to fix the meal.

Now, referring to the second time chart, work backwards from the serving time and decide when everything needs to be started so dinner will be ready (and cleaned up) at the same time!

When gaps or waiting periods appear in your schedule, tuck in small jobs like assembling the relish tray, setting the table, and spot cleanups. Be sure everything on the menu list and the non-food list is accounted for.

8:00 a.m. Make stuffing (may also be made day ahead but do not stuff turkey until baking time).

8:20 a.m. Prepare and stuff turkey

8:30 a.m. Turkey into oven, vegetable relishes prepared, potatoes peeled—cover with ice water until needed

8:45 a.m. Cleanup

10:00 a.m. Make rolls, cleanup (may also be made day ahead)

11:45 a.m. Shape rolls

12:45 p.m. Set table; set out dessert dishes and serving pieces

1:00 p.m. Relish tray assembled, unmold salad, dish cranberry sauce, cleanup

1:10 p.m. Potatoes on to cook

1:15 p.m. Prepare sweet potato casserole and green bean casserole

1:30 p.m. Turkey out, casseroles and rolls in oven, make gravy

1:40 p.m. Potatoes off—mash (warm in oven), cleanup

1:40 p.m. Jim—Carve turkey, dish stuffing

2:00 p.m. Serve

Notice that there are several cleanup points included in this schedule. Though it sounds tedious, each cleanup requires only a few minutes. Things are so much easier to clean when they are handled immediately. The longer a dish sits around, the longer it takes to clean. After-meal cleanup is greatly simplified when you only have to deal with the dishes and serving pieces. The more pots, pans, and mixing bowls you have lying around, the more complicated cleaning up will be.

For those of you who are already efficient meal-managers, these steps are routine and automatic to you. For those of you who struggle, follow these steps and soon you, too, will be able to serve any meal on time and in a *clean* kitchen!

15

The Magic of Mixes

If you glance through your kitchen cupboards, chances are you will see an assortment of mixes. Our active lifestyle has created a need for these timesaving convenience foods. With the aid of a few *homemade* mixes, you can put a nutritious meal on the table in the shortest amount of time without slaving away in the kitchen.

Even when you want to provide a hearty farmhouse meal or a delicacy for a discriminating gourmet, mixes can make kitchen hours reasonable. Mixes save time. Mixes are tremendously handy especially during those hours when time is at a premium. The time-consuming part of cooking is mainly the get ready and the clean up when you assemble and put away equipment and ingredients. Mixes give you accrued benefits every time. One get ready and one clean up will give you several timesaving meals.

To fully enjoy the benefits of mixes, consider making your own.

1. Homemade mixes are more economical than packaged goods. Why pay extra for someone else's labor and for costly packaging?

2. Homemade mixes are more nutritious. You can enjoy the convenience while you control the quality. Ingredients you combine at home will likely be fresher than store purchased mixes. They will also be free from additives and preservatives, an important consideration these days. Also, with your own mixes you can still enjoy that "I made it all by myself" feeling you get when you prepare something from scratch.

3. Homemade mixes are versatile and can be tailored to your family's taste. Their wide variety of uses makes this a real strong point. Mixes are used well in baking, seasonings, sauces, and main dishes. The possibilities are unlimited.

Following are some specific ideas to get you started. This is only a sampling of what is possible when you discover the magic of mixes. Check your favorite bookstore or library for homemade mix cookbooks. Watch the pages of women's magazines. Because of their increasing popularity, homemade mix recipes are becoming easier to find.

As you read through these recipes, keep in mind these are only examples. I have tried to select versatile recipes that I feel can be of the most general use.

Let's begin with the age-old standard, ground beef. Whenever possible, buy fresh ground beef in large quantities and prepare it in several different ways. First, make what I call "basic ground beef." Brown several pounds of hamburger with onion, celery, and green pepper (optional). Drain the fat and freeze the cooked ground beef in two and one half-cup portions. Whenever a recipe calls for browned hamburger, pull one of your containers from the freezer and you've got browned hamburger, without any mess and/or time. By browning the hamburger all at once, you've eliminated the duplication of getting ready and cleaning up.

Just think of all the dishes you use hamburger in: chili, sloppy joes, tacos, spaghetti, and a myriad of casseroles. The list goes on and on. Imagine the time you could save just by having basic ground beef on hand.

While the world isn't waiting for another hamburger recipe, here's one I can't resist sharing with you. Did you know that you can make spaghetti in one pan? Here's how: In a large pan, put one container of basic ground beef, Italian spice mix (from your favorite spaghetti recipe, or you can use my recipe at the end of this chapter as a guide), one teaspoon of salt, and forty-six ounces of tomato juice. Bring to a boil, then add six ounces of spaghetti and cook until tender.

The spaghetti thickens the sauce as it cooks. This recipe can be completely done in about fifteen minutes. One word of caution: if you find you've put in too much spaghetti and the sauce is getting super thick, just thin it with a little water or tomato juice.

BASIC GROUND BEEF MIX

1 lb. ground beef
½ cup chopped onion
½ cup chopped celery
¼ cup chopped green pepper (optional)

In a heavy skillet, cook ground beef with vegetables until meat is browned and vegetables are tender. Drain fat, cool and freeze in approximately 2-cup portions. Use in any recipe calling for browned ground beef. Multiply this recipe and have several containers of Basic Ground Beef in freezer.

CHILI CASSEROLE

1 container Basic Ground Beef
1 pkg. chili seasoning mix*
8-oz can tomato sauce
2/3 cup water
1-lb. can kidney beans, undrained
4 oz. corn chips
1/4 cup sliced, pitted black olives
grated cheese

In large saucepan, mix Basic Ground Beef, seasoning mix, tomato sauce, and water. Heat for 15 minutes. In greased 9x13 casserole, layer meat, beans, chips, olives, and cheese. Bake at 350° for 30 minutes or until cheese melts and casserole is hot. Makes approximately 8 servings. * May substitute Mexican Seasoning Mix—recipe follows.
Menu Mates: Tossed salad; chilled, sliced peaches.

QUICK CHILI

1 container Basic Ground Beef
2 1-lb. cans kidney beans, undrained
1/2 cup chopped onion
32-oz. can tomatoes
10 1/2-oz. can tomato soup
1/4 teaspoon garlic powder
1 1/2 tablespoon chili powder
2 teaspoons salt

In large saucepan, combine all ingredients. Cook until onions are tender and chili is hot. Makes approximately 6 servings.
Menu Mates: Crisp crackers, dill pickles, cheese slices, finger salad.

UPSIDE-DOWN PIE

1 container Basic Ground Beef
1/2 teaspoon salt

10½-oz. can tomato soup
1½ cup biscuit dough
1 cup grated cheddar cheese

Preheat oven to 450° F. Prepare biscuit dough as directed later in this chapter. Set aside. In saucepan, combine Basic Ground Beef, salt, and soup. When mixture is hot, pour into a 9-inch pie plate. Roll biscuit dough into a 10-inch circle and place on top of the meat mixture. Bake for 15 minutes. Invert pie onto a large plate. Sprinkle with cheese. Makes approximately 6 servings.
Menu Mates: Buttered lima beans, sliced strawberries and bananas.

BAKED BEANS AND HAMBURGER

1 container, Basic Ground Beef, thawed
30-oz. can pork and beans
8-oz can tomato sauce
2 tablespoons vinegar
1 teaspoon prepared mustard
2 tablespoons brown sugar

In large casserole, combine ingredients and bake at 350° F. for 30 minutes. Makes approximately 6 to 8 servings.
Menu Mates: Coleslaw, jelly muffins, fruit ambrosia.

HAMBURGER MACARONI AND CHEESE

7¼-oz. package macaroni and cheese dinner
1 container Basic Ground Beef, thawed

Prepare macaroni and cheese as package directs. Add Basic Ground Beef and heat thoroughly. Makes approximately 4 to 6 servings.
Menu Mates: Tossed salad with fresh spinach, fresh or canned fruit cocktail.

BEEF AND RICE

1 container Basic Ground Beef
1¾ cup water

1 cup uncooked Minute Rice
10½-oz. can cream of chicken soup
10-oz. pkg frozen peas
¼ teaspoon salt

In large saucepan, combine all ingredients. Bring mixture to a
boil. Cover and reduce heat. Cook for 15 minutes. Makes approximately 6 servings.
Menu Mates: Sliced tomatoes and cucumbers, tapioca pudding
with pineapple.

ONE-DISH DINNER

4 oz. noodles
1 container Basic Ground Beef
catsup
10½ can tomato soup
1-lb. can creamed corn

Cook noodles in boiling, salted water as package directs. Meanwhile, combine Basic Ground Beef, soup, and corn in large
saucepan. When noodles are tender, drain and combine with
meat mixture. Add catsup to taste. Heat thoroughly (or bake in
350° F. oven for 30 to 45 minutes). Makes approximately 6
servings.
Menu Mates: Lettuce wedges, carrot sticks, gelatin fruit mold.

TATER TOT
CASSEROLE

1 container Basic Ground Beef, thawed
10½ oz. can cream of mushroom soup
½ cup milk
½ lb. tater tots
1 can french-fried onions

Cover bottom of 9x9-inch baking pan with Basic Ground Beef. In
small bowl, combine soup and milk. Mix well and pour over
meat mixture. Place tater tots on top of casserole and bake at
350° F. for 35 minutes. Remove from oven and spread 1 can onions on top of potatoes. Return to oven and bake 10 minutes
longer. Makes approximately 6 servings.

Next, use several more pounds of fresh hamburger to make up
meatloaves. You can use the basic meatloaf mix for meatloaf variations and for all your meatloaf recipes. Divide the prepared meat-

loaf mixture into one and one-half pound meatloaves and freeze them in aluminum foil. Whenever you want plain meatloaf for dinner, take one from the freezer and bake it. If you're serving a filled meatloaf, defrost the meatloaf, fill, and bake it.

When making a recipe that calls for meatballs, defrost a meatloaf and make it up into meatballs. (Sometimes when I'm making the meatloaf mix, I make up several batches of meatballs and bake them in the oven, cool, and freeze. This, however, can limit your variations by forcing you to have a certain number of meals using meatballs.)

BASIC MEATLOAF AND MEATBALL MIX

1 cup milk
3 slices soft bread
¼ teaspoon each pepper, dry mustard, sage, celery salt, and
   garlic salt
1 egg, beaten
1½ lbs. ground beef
1¼ teaspoon salt
1 tablespoon Worcestershire sauce

Pour milk into a large mixing bowl. Tear up bread into small pieces and soak in milk. Add remaining ingredients and mix well. Form into loaf (or desired shape). Bake at 350° F. for 1 to 1½ hours. Makes one 1½ meatloaf. Multiply ingredients and make several unbaked meatloaves for the freezer. Wrap individual meatloaves in heavy-duty foil.
Menu Mates: Twice baked potatoes; glazed, cooked carrots; Waldorf salad.

FILLED BEEF ROLL

1 Meatloaf Mix, thawed
1 cup cooked rice
½ cup grated swiss cheese
2 tablespoons chopped green pepper

Roll thawed Meatloaf Mix into a 10x8 inch rectangle. In small bowl combine rice, cheese, and green pepper. Pat rice mixture onto meatloaf leaving 1-inch margins all around. Roll up jelly

roll style. Seal side ends and seams by pressing meat edges together. Bake at 350° F. for 35 minutes. Makes approximately 6
servings.
Menu Mates: Spinach, pineapple cottage cheese salad, corn muffins.

CHEESE MEATLOAF

1 Meatloaf Mix, thawed
1 egg white
¼ lb. grated Cheddar or crumbled Bleu cheese
1 tablespoon water
2 slices bread

Pat ½ of Meatloaf Mix into a greased 9x5x3-inch loaf pan. Combine slightly beaten egg white and water. Tear bread into tiny
pieces, toss with egg white and water. Add cheese and mix by
tossing gently. Cover meat with cheese mixture; top with rest of
meat. Bake at 350° F. for 1½ hours. Makes approximately 6
servings.
Menu Mates: Buttered green beans, gelatin fruit salad, biscuits.

MEATLOAF SAUCE

¼ catsup
1 teaspoon dry mustard
2 tablespoons brown sugar

Combine all ingredients in a small saucepan. Bring to a boil,
stirring. Spread sauce on top of meatloaf the last 15 minutes of
baking.

GRAPE JELLY
MEATBALLS
(Sounds awful, tastes fantastic!)

1 Meatball Mix
10 oz. (about ¾ cup) grape jelly
12 oz. chili sauce

Shape thawed meatloaf mixture into 1 tablespoon meatballs. Set
aside. In large saucepan, mix chili sauce and grape jelly. Heat,

stirring until well blended. Add RAW meatballs to sauce. Cover and simmer one hour. (When you put the meatballs into the sauce you're probably going to think that something is wrong because the sauce is so scarce. As the meatballs cook, the sauce increases greatly from the meat juices.) When meatballs have simmered for 10 to 15 minutes, stir occasionally during cooking. Makes about 4 dozen Grape Jelly Meatballs. (The sauce can be served over rice, when desired.)

Menu Mates: Potatoes au gratin, gelatin fruit salad, asparagus tips on tomato slices.

OVEN BAKED MEATBALLS

Prepare meatloaf recipe as directed above. Shape mixture into 1-inch balls. Place meatballs in ungreased shallow baking pan. Bake at 350° F. for 10 to 15 minutes or until meatballs are browned. 4 lbs. of meatloaf mix will make approximately 144 meatballs (12 dozen). For freezing, put about 30 meatballs each into 5 one-quart containers.

NOTE: Rather than shape individual meatballs, try this: Place meatloaf mixture in 15½x10½-inch jelly roll pan. Pat mixture into 10x6 inch rectangle. Cut into 1-inch squares. Slightly separate squares. Bake at 350° F. for 15 minutes or until browned. Makes approximately 54-60 meatball squares.

BARBEQUE SAUCE FOR MEATBALLS

1 cup catsup
½ cup chili sauce
¼ cup brown sugar
4 teaspoons Worcestershire sauce
2 tablespoons butter
¼ cup chopped onion
2 tablespoons prepared mustard
1/4 teaspoon garlic salt

In large saucepan, combine all ingredients. Bring to a boil, stirring until smooth and sugar is dissolved. Add 1 one quart container baked meatballs and heat through. Makes approximately 6 servings.

Menu Mates: Hard rolls with butter, potato chips, crisp relishes, fresh fruit and cheese.

MEATBALL STROGANOFF

1 cup chopped onion
1/4 cup butter
3 tablespoons flour
1/8 teaspoon garlic powder
1/8 teaspoon pepper
1 tablespoon catsup
10 1/2 can condensed beef bouillon
1/4 cup water
1 quart baked meatballs
1 1/2 cup sour cream

In large saucepan, cook onion in butter until onions are tender but not brown. Stir in flour. Add garlic powder, pepper, catsup, bouillon and water. Cook and stir until mixture bubbles. Add meatballs and cook over low heat (10 minutes for thawed meatballs, or 20 minutes frozen). Stir occasionally while meatballs are heating. Mix in sour cream. Heat, but do not boil. Serve over cooked rice or noodles. Makes approximately 6 to 8 servings.
Menu Mates: Deviled green beans, lettuce wedges with dressing.

Finally, make up a bunch of hamburger patties. Place one layer of patties on a cookie sheet and freeze. As soon as hamburgers are completely frozen, store in freezer wrap or freezer containers. After the hamburgers are frozen, they will not stick together, allowing you to use just the number of hamburgers needed.

Rather than the quick-freeze method, patties can be formed then separated by a piece of wax paper or plactic wrap. Stack, wrap, and freeze.

Presweetened drink mix cans (for large hamburgers) or Pringle's potato chip cans (for small hamburgers) are the perfect size for storing frozen hamburgers. When both ends of the can are removed and replaced with plastic lids, the hamburgers can be pushed right out, one at a time.

When I'm in a hurry I spread the hamburger in a large cookie sheet with sides. Using a rolling pin, the meat is pressed firmly into the pan. Then I take a sharp knife and cut the meat into approximately three-inch squares. I remove each individual patty from the pan and I've got a bunch of square hamburgers. I figure if square hamburgers are good enough for Wendy's, they're good enough for me!

If you frequently prepare chicken dishes, you can eliminate a lot of getting ready with this idea. Imagine the time you'd save preparing chicken dishes if you have packages of cut-up cooked chicken in your freezer. If you buy chicken in quantity, you can cook the chicken, remove the bones (if desired), and freeze several three-cup portions at one time. (If you boil the chicken, don't forget to freeze and label the broth, also.)

CHICKEN (OR TURKEY) DIVAN

2 10-oz. pkgs. broccoli
1 container cooked chicken, thawed
6 slices American cheese (or 1 cup grated cheese)
14½-oz. can evaporated milk
10½-oz. can cream of mushroom soup
1 can french-fried onions

Cook broccoli according to package directions. Put broccoli into oblong baking dish and cover with chicken. Top with cheese. In small bowl, combine milk and soup. Pour over entire casserole. Bake at 350° F. for 25 minutes. Cover with onions and bake 5 minutes more. Makes approximately 6 servings.
Menu Mates: Pear halves filled with cranberry sauce, brown and serve rolls.

QUICK CHICKEN CASSEROLE

1 container cooked chicken, thawed
1 10 oz. pkg. frozen mixed vegetables, thawed
1 10½ oz. can cream of chicken soup
½ cup milk
1 can french fried onions

In mixing bowl, combine chicken, mixed vegetables, soup, and milk. Mix well. Add 1 cup french fried onions and pour into 1½ quart baking dish. Cover. Bake at 375° F. for 40 minutes. Uncover and top with remaining onions. Bake 5 minutes more. Makes approximately 6 servings.
Menu Mates: Orange-walnut muffins, chilled applesauce.

CHICKEN CHOP SUEY
(Easier than it looks!)

2 tablespoons butter
1 cup sliced celery
1/4 cup chopped onion
10 1/2-oz. can cream of mushroom soup
1 cup milk
2 tablespoons soy sauce
1/8 teaspoon Tabasco sauce
1/2 teaspoon salt
1 container cooked chicken
1-lb can bean sprouts, drained
1/2 cup sour cream
cooked rice
chopped salted cashews

In large skillet, melt butter. Sauté celery and onion 5 minutes.
In small bowl combine soup, milk, soy sauce, Tabasco sauce, and
salt. Put chicken and bean sprouts in skillet and add soup mix-
ture. Cover and simmer 15 to 20 minutes. Stir in sour cream.
Heat, but do not boil. Serve over hot rice. Top with cashews.
Makes approximately 6 to 8 servings.
Menu Mates: Snow peas; salad of melon balls, banana, pineapple
chunks, and seedless grapes.

Spice up your recipes with your own seasoning mixes. You can
duplicate these recipes or make up your own.

Using my favorite spaghetti recipe, I make up individual Italian
seasoning packets. I put six or eight juice glasses on my kitchen
counter and line each glass with a plastic sandwich bag. Then, I get
out the ingredients called for in the recipe. Into each bag I put two
tablespoons instant minced onion, one-fourth teaspoon garlic powder, two tablespoons parsley flakes, etc. A sandwich-size freezer
container holds several seasoning packets. The container is labeled with masking tape.

The same idea works well with homemade salad dressing seasonings, taco seasoning mix, sloppy joe and chili seasoning mix,
etc. It's a good idea to make up seasoning packets for anything that
you make frequently. There are times when I enjoy making things

from scratch using fresh onions, parsley, and garlic, but there are times when I'd rather save time!

ITALIAN SPICE MIX

2 tablespoons instant minced onion
1 teaspoon salt
2 tablespoons parsley flakes
1/4 teaspoons dried thyme leaves, crushed
1/4 teaspoon garlic powder
1 tablespoon brown sugar
1 bay leaf
1 1/2 teaspoons dried oregano, crushed

Mix ingredients and store. This makes one packet of spice mix. I use this blend for anything Italian; pizza, spaghetti, lasagne, manicotti, etc.

MEXICAN SEASONING MIX

1 cup instant minced onion
2/3 cup instant beef bouillon
1/3 cup chili powder
2 tablespoons ground cumin
4 teaspoons each crushed red pepper and oregano
2 teaspoons garlic powder

Mix ingredients thoroughly and store in tightly covered container. Use 3 tablespoons with 1/2 cup water to every pound of meat in chili or tacos.

Round out your meals with a fruit or vegetable gelatin salad. Here's how you can even make your own gelatin!

DO-IT-YOURSELF GELATIN FOR SALADS OR DESSERTS

1 tablespoon unflavored gelatin
1/3-1/2 cup sugar
1/2 teaspoon unsweetened drink mix

In small bowl, mix dry ingredients thoroughly. Dissolve in one cup boiling water. Stir until dissolved. Add one cup cold water. Chill until firm.

A homemade biscuit mix is extremely versatile. It can help you prepare the kind of breakfasts you thought you'd never have time for! It can even help put a quick finishing touch on dinner!

BUTTERMILK BAKING MIX

10½ cups sifted flour
¼ cup baking powder
1½ tablespoons salt
½ cup sugar
2 cups shortening
1 cup buttermilk powder
2½ teaspoons baking soda

In a large bowl, mix all ingredients with an electric mixer until particles are small and uniform in size. Store on a shelf in a tightly covered container. Makes 13 cups mix. Storage life is approximately 3 months.

BUTTERMILK PANCAKES

2 cups Baking Mix
1⅔ cups milk
1 egg

In mixing bowl, combine all the ingredients and beat until smooth. (If thinner pancakes are desired, add more milk.) Slowly heat griddle or heavy skillet. When using an electric griddle, preheat to 400° F. To test temperature, put a small amount of cold water onto hot griddle; water should roll off in drops. Use about ¼ cup batter for each pancake. Cook until bubbles form on the surface and edges become dry. Turn and cook until nicely browned. Makes eighteen 4-inch pancakes.

When time and energy permit, try these pancake treats the kids will love: Drop pancake batter onto hot griddle one tablespoon at a time and fill the griddle with tiny mouthful size "silver dollar" pancakes. For pancakes the children will really eat up, pour the batter onto a heated griddle in the shape of their initials, or, if you are really creative, animals.

BUTTERMILK WAFFLES

2 cups Baking Mix
1 egg
1²/₃ cups milk
2 tablespoons salad oil

Preheat waffle iron. Meanwhile, combine ingredients and beat until mixture is smooth. For each waffle, pour batter into center of lower half of greased or nonstick waffle iron, until it spreads to 1 inch from the edge. Bake until waffle stops steaming (or follow manufacturer's instructions). Makes 2 large or 6 small waffles.

BUTTERMILK CHIFFON WAFFLES

2 eggs, separated
1 cup milk
¼ cup salad oil
2¹/₃ cups Baking Mix
2 tablespoons sugar

Preheat waffle iron. In small bowl, with rotary beater, beat egg whites until soft peaks form when beater is raised. In medium bowl, beat egg yolks, milk, and salad oil until well combined. Gradually add Baking Mix and sugar. Beat until smooth. With rubber spatula, fold egg whites into batter, just until combined (leave a few fluffs). For each waffle, pour batter into center of lower half of greased or nonstick waffle iron until it spreads to 1 inch from edge. Bake until waffle stops steaming (or follow manufacturer's instructions). Makes 2 large or 6 small waffles.

Pancakes and waffles are especially delicious when served with Honey Maple Syrup.

HONEY MAPLE SYRUP

4½ cups sugar
3 cups water
1½ teaspoons maple flavor (or to taste)
2¼ cup light corn syrup
¾ cup honey
¾ teaspoon butter flavor

Combine all ingredients in saucepan. Cook and stir until sugar is dissolved. This recipe makes about ½ gallon. Store in a covered container in the refrigerator.

At dinner, the Buttermilk Baking Mix comes to the rescue again, helping you serve a few quick extras.

BUTTERMILK BISCUITS

2 cups Baking Mix
⅔ cup milk

Preheat oven to 450° F. In mixing bowl, combine baking mix and milk. Stir with fork until the mixture becomes a soft dough. Beat the buttermilk dough 15 strokes. The dough will be stiff and sticky. Knead dough 8 to 10 times until smooth. Roll out the dough until it is ½ inch thick. Cut with floured biscuit cutter. Bake on ungreased baking sheet for 10 to 15 minutes. This recipe makes twelve 2-inch biscuits.

BUTTERMILK MUFFINS

2 cups Baking Mix
1 egg
2 tablespoons sugar
¾ cup milk

Heat oven to 400° F. In mixing bowl, blend ingredients and beat for 30 seconds. Grease well 12 muffin cups and fill ⅔ full. Bake for 15 minutes.

JELLY MUFFINS

Follow basic muffin recipe above. Grease 12 muffin cups. Put 2 tablespoons batter in each muffin cup. Put 1 teaspoon jam, jelly or preserves on top. Pour remaining batter in each muffin cup, filling ⅔ full.

ORANGE WALNUT MUFFINS

Follow basic muffin recipe above adding 1 tablespoon grated orange peel and ⅓ cup chopped walnuts to dry ingredients. Proceed as directed.

BLUEBERRY MUFFINS

Follow basic muffin recipe above, increasing sugar to ⅓ cup. To dry ingredients add 1 cup fresh blueberries or ¾ cup canned or thawed frozen blueberries (drained well). Proceed as directed.

RAISIN MUFFINS

Follow basic muffin recipe above, adding 1 tablespoon grated orange peel and ½ cup seedless raisins to dry ingredients. Proceed as directed.

APRICOT MUFFINS

Follow basic muffin recipe above, adding 2 teaspoons grated orange peel and ½ cup finely chopped dried apricots to dry ingredients. Proceed as directed.

When you've got the time and energy, the Buttermilk Baking Mix can speed you through a myriad of dessert preparations. Here are a few ideas that'll make you a hit for sure.

BANANA CARAMEL BISCUITS

½ cup butter, melted
½ cup packed brown sugar
1 teaspoon cinnamon
2 cups Baking Mix
2 small ripe mashed bananas

In small saucepan, melt butter. Meanwhile, combine brown sugar and cinnamon in small bowl. Set aside. In mixing bowl, combine Baking Mix and bananas. Knead until well blended. Put a teaspoon melted butter in each of 12 muffin cups; sprinkle a teaspoon of the brown sugar, cinnamon mixture in each of the 12 muffin cups. Roll kneaded dough into a 12-inch rectangle. Spread dough with remaining butter and sprinkle with remaining bown sugar and cinnamon. Roll up dough from long side of rectangle in jelly-roll fashion. Cut into 12 rolls. Place cut side down in muffin cups. Bake 10 to 12 minutes at 450° F. Do not overbake.

PUDDING COOKIES

¾ cup Baking Mix
¼ cup salad oil
1 egg
1 small pkg. instant pudding
2 tablespoons sugar

Heat oven to 350° F. In mixing bowl, combine all ingredients. Mix until dough forms a ball. Shape into small balls using 1 teaspoon dough for each ball. Place on ungreased baking sheet. With a floured fork, flatten balls to about 2 inches in diameter. Bake 8 minutes. Makes about 2½ dozen cookies.

PEANUT BUTTER COOKIES

1 cup peanut butter
¼ cup shortening
1 cup sugar or packed brown sugar
½ cup boiling water
2 cups Baking Mix

Heat oven to 400° F. In mixing bowl, blend peanut butter, shortening, sugar, and water until smooth. Stir in Baking Mix and drop teaspoonfuls on lightly greased baking sheet. Flatten each cookie with a floured fork. Bake 8 to 10 minutes. Makes about 5 dozen cookies.

CHOCOLATE CHIP COOKIES

1/4 cup soft butter
3/4 cup packed brown sugar
1 egg
1 1/3 cups Baking Mix
1/2 cup chopped nuts
1 cup semisweet chocolate chips

Preheat oven to 375° F. In mixing bowl, beat butter, sugar, and egg until light and fluffy. Stir in Baking Mix, nuts, and chocolate chips. Drop onto ungreased baking sheet. Bake 10 minutes or until light brown. Makes about 2 dozen cookies.

May I share just one more timesaving recipe? I got this one from my dad, Fred Wheeler, who spent his working life in bakery research. I'm not sure whether I get more satisfaction from the recipe or from knowing that it's from my dad.

Whenever you have a cookie or cake recipe that calls for a greased and floured pan, try this recipe for cookie and cake pan grease. With this little dandy on hand, you can grease and flour a pan in one operation. It is also less expensive than commercial products now on the market.

COOKIE AND CAKE PAN GREASE

2 cups shortening
1 1/2 cups unsifted flour

With electric mixer, mix ingredients thoroughly. Store in a covered container. Use within three months.

When you've come to the end of another exhausting day, put

your feet up and relax with a piping hot cup of Quick Hot Chocolate.

HOT CHOCOLATE MIX

2 cups granulated sugar
3½ tablespoons pure vanilla extract
5 cups powdered sugar
10½ cups noninstant milk powder
2½ cups cocoa
1½ teaspoons salt

Put granulated sugar in a large bowl. Add vanilla extract. With your hands, rub the sugar and vanilla together until sugar is uniform in color. Gradually, add powdered sugar and continue rubbing until all sugar is mixed in. Add milk, cocoa, and salt and mix well. Sift entire mixture and store in covered container. Add 3 heaping teaspoonfuls of mixture to one cup hot water for delicious hot chocolate.

Once you have tried a few mixes, the time you'll save will motivate you to further experimentation. It is not necessary to use these exact recipes. With a little experience, you can use your own recipes and make up your own mixes.

Again I am not suggesting that you have ground beef, chicken, and biscuits every night. These are just the most universally used foods; therefore, these ideas will be able to streamline most everyone's kitchen hours.

On days when time is low and nerves are high a mix can save your day. When you have a leisurely day and want to cook everything from scratch, you still have that option.

There are a lot of times when I enjoy spending time in my kitchen making everything from scratch, but I also like having these mixes handy. With mixes you can have the best of both worlds.

Commit yourself to making one mix this week. Start cashing in on those accrued benefits. After you've tried it, I guarantee you'll be a convert to a whole new way of life!

16

Turning Toyland Into Joyland

When our first baby was born, I couldn't believe how much room that little guy took up. Blankets, quilts, diapers, high chair, and changing table took an extensive toll of our available space. What I didn't realize was that it would get worse fast! A quilt can be folded neatly and placed on a closet shelf, but what do you do with the dried corn cobs your little boy likes to push around with his bulldozer?

I know a woman who hadn't seen one of her daughter's dresses for weeks. One day it was unearthed under three feet of debris on the closet floor. Believe me, I can understand. I've learned from experience that three thousand baseball cards can hide almost anything.

Then, there's the car. When we travel with the children, I usually arrive at our destination sitting cross-legged, Indian fashion, in the front seat. The reason for the Lotus position is because the car floor is heaped so high with trash, shoes, toys, crayons, and half-eaten hamburgers there is no room for my feet!

As you can see, toys and assorted wreckage have caused more home-management problems than unemployment. If you are wringing your hands wondering what to do, the best way to spell relief is O-R-G-A-N-I-Z-E. But where do you start? The hard part about organizing your kids' stuff is that your offspring are usually unorganizing faster than you can organize.

But, don't fret. Let's get started in the toy department and put an end to some of this disorganization.

Do you put all your kids' toys into a toybox and wonder why they never play with their toys? Or do you spend hours making toy bags and feel frustrated when your kids dump everything out to find what they want.

TOYBOX TERRORS

As soon as our number one child got old enough to play and began to accumulate a collection of toys, we rushed right out and got him a toybox. Every child had to have a toybox, I thought. But things were always a mess in that toybox, and I couldn't stand it. I tried to organize it, putting cars and trucks here, building blocks there, but to no avail. Every evening I was on my knees in front of the toybox—not praying for help (which I obviously needed), but rearranging and putting things back in place. It drove me nuts!

Next, I tried storage alternative number one—hanging (no, not myself, although there were days . . .). Thinking there had to be a workable solution to this confusion, I sat right down and sewed up a bunch of drawstring toy bags. I sorted and categorized each group of toys (again) into a separate bag and hung them up in the toy closet. Feeling much like Betsy Ross must have felt after finishing the flag, I stood back to admire my toy bag creations.

Then came the true test—children. The toy bags were hard for them to handle, and in order to choose a specific toy, they had to dump everything on the floor.

Next, I tried shelving. Here's where I found the storage alternative that worked best for us.

I got an old bookshelf and organized toys on the shelves. Again, dishpans came to the rescue. I had a dishpan for each of the following: Legos, Lincoln logs, small vehicles, building and puzzle blocks, dolls and accessories, guns and cowboy gear. Smaller things were contained in rectangular-shaped planters (about the size of half a dishpan), made out of heavy plastic. Things like small cowboys and Indians, soldiers, spacemen, little people, animals, furniture, and so on, went into these containers.

Plastic ice-cream pails would work well, too. They can also be hung from hooks. However, as with any round container, they waste space. So, if you're short on space avoid anything round. One added feature of the ice cream pails, though—they are free!

Each toy container was labeled with a permanent black marker so we'd know what belonged where. Hand-drawn pictures or pictures cut from magazines could also be used to identify the contents of the container for the youngsters who do not read. They should also know where things belong.

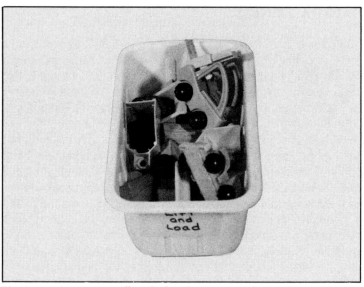

Plastic containers are excellent for keeping toys organized and accessible

I had two rectangular laundry baskets. One was used to hold large vehicles. the other was used for large adventure-set things which were always used together.

Now, every little thing has a place. When we see something out of place, we can quickly put it into its proper container. Although the kids will occasionally dump out the contents of a container, they can usually choose just the toy they want.

Remember, you don't need a bookcase or built-in shelves for toys. Shelves can be built with particle board and stacked bricks, cement blocks, or large cans of food. Right now in our home, we have some shelves made from particle board and honey cans! Inexpensive snap-together metal shelves or sturdy cardboard shelves can be purchased at any discount store. They come in many different sizes.

You don't need to have fancy, expensive equipment to get organized. Use your imagination and try to make do with the space available to you. If we could always remember to make the most of our resources, we would all be much happier.

My in-depth research (through trial and error) led me to discover the best storage alternative for me. I learned something along the way, though. Each of the storage alternatives for toys has different advantages. To help you choose what will work best for you (without so much trial and error) let's consider the pluses and minuses of each option.

THE FOUR STORAGE ALTERNATIVES FOR TOYS

The most obvious storage method is, of course, the toybox. The toybox has a few marked advantages. First of all, it can be decorative, adding to the overall look of a room. It also keeps the toys hidden from view, which makes the room more pleasing to the eye. Toyboxes usually require only a small amount of floor space, which may be a prime consideration for those living in cramped quarters.

Some toyboxes depending on the shape provide a perfect storage area for bats, balls, and otherwise cumbersome equipment.

However, the toybox usually becomes a hollow space in which to dump any given number of things. In order to make a toybox system truly functional, the toys need to be grouped and divided so the children can find and use what they want. Keeping the system going requires daily maintenance.

Sometimes a standard toybox is not large enough to accommodate all the toys, so an additional storage method has to be used. (Drawers, by the way, have the same advantages and disadvantages as toy boxes.)

Another common storage alternative is the toy bag. These are bags with drawstring openings made from any kind of fabric. The bags can be made from a fabric that coordinates with the room decoration. With words or pictures, the bags can be labeled so the children will know what is contained inside. A clear plastic "window" can also be sewn on the bag so the child can get a better view.

The bags are usually kept hanging on an available wall or other vertical space. Because they are stored in a hanging position, they can make use of what would otherwise be wasted space. Saving space, then, would be a positive benefit from toy bags. Another benefit is that they cannot be easily dumped by toddlers.

In my opinion, toy bags have several disadvantages. My main objection is that they are hard to handle. When a bag contains

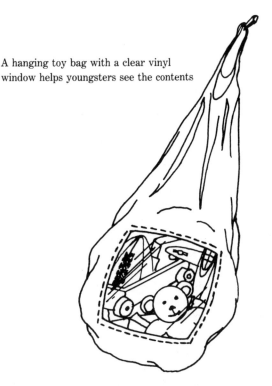

A hanging toy bag with a clear vinyl
window helps youngsters see the contents

small vehicles, for example, it's hard for a child to get "The General Lee" (or other favorite car) without pouring the contents of the bag on the floor. Toy bags are better suited for complete toy sets that are always used together, not separately.

Also, it is difficult for a child to put toys back into a toy bag. He has to hold the bag with one hand while the other little hand drops a few things at a time into the bag's opening. Once the bags are hanging it is sometimes awkward to put a stray, forgotten piece back in.

So, toy bags can be decorative, they can save space and they can be kept out of the reach of young children. However, they are hard to handle and will require extra time when toys are put away.

The last storage alternative is shelving. Using this method the toys are categorized and put into dishpans, ice cube bins, cardboard boxes, laundry baskets—preferably anything square or rectangular in shape. Plastic ice-cream pails are free, though, and have lids that can be used to discourage those little toddlers. They can also be hung up. That way you get one-motion storage by easily selecting just what they want without dropping things out on the floor. It is extremely easy to sort and return toys to their respective cartons, again using one motion.

Open shelves of toys are not decorative and add to the cluttered look of an area, so they are best kept in a closet or behind a screen or blind.

Learn from my mistakes. Weigh the advantages and disadvantages of each toy storage method and choose the right one for you.

MORE TOY STORAGE IDEAS

After buying the toybox, the next thing we purchased for our firstborn was a small bookcase. We bought him scores of books (of course he had to be the brightest child on the block) and we needed someplace to keep them. With the books on a bookshelf, all the child could see were these nondescript, thin spines. There they were, fifty books looking pretty much the same. The only way he could pick out a book was to deposit them all over the floor.

Frustrated again, I struck gold. I bought a heavy plastic kitty-litter pan (a shallow corrugated box would also work) and put it on the closet floor. There I stood the books in the pan with the covers facing forward. The pan is wide enough for two rows of small books side by side. A child can look through the books without having to disturb them. His selection is easy and the bright, illustrated book covers act as invitations to read. (And best news of all is that kitty-litter pans now come in decorator colors!!)

You may need more than one box, and maybe you'd like to keep your box of books on a shelf. I chose the floor because there was no place else for his books to go, and even a small child could easily use the book collection. So many times over the years I've seen one of our children curled up in a corner by the floor library looking at a book.

This same idea can be used for your older children's LP stereo records. The kitty pan (as well as some dishpans) will confine the

A kitty litter pan keeps children's books tidy and easy for young readers to use

Record albums and book and record sets are organized and orderly when stored like this

records, and by standing them up, the record jackets are easy to see and records are easy to select.

Ice-cube bins are durable containers that can be used to organize a number of things. For your child's coloring-book collection, stand the coloring books in a dishpan, and in front of the coloring books put an ice-cube bin to hold crayons, scissors, markers, etc. When your child wants to color, he can grab the dishpan and have everything he needs in a portable container. Ice-cube bins are also good receptacles for book and record sets. Or you can use the bins as toy organizers on your toy shelf.

Coloring books and crayons stored in their own ready-to-color dishpan

Now, with things organized, our kids spend more time playing with their *toys*, instead of the box they came in!

WHERE SHOULD THE TOYS BE KEPT?

The most important basic organizing principle regarding toys is *grouping*—having one central location for *all* of the toys. Ideally, this central location should not be in a child's bedroom (particularly if there is more than one child in the family).

Let's say Jim has his toys stored in his room and Mary has hers stored in her room. Here's what usually happens. When Jim's room is "totaled" everyone simply packs up and moves to Mary's room. Shortly, Mary's room is in as bad a shape as Jim's. The toys (Jim's and Mary's) are scrambled together and mixed up. When cleaning time inevitably rolls around you have to sort the toys by ownership before they can be returned to their rightful places.

It's so much faster and easier to put all the blocks in one bin and all the crayons in another. If you expect other people to help you keep things in order, eliminate as many decisions and movements as you can. In other words, make your system simple. Which sounds easier? Running from room to room distributing a few toys here and a few toys there; or, gathering all the toys and depositing them in one central area?

Another reason for not keeping toys in a bedroom is that toys add to the cluttered look of a room. It is especially important for children that their room has a neat appearance. When things always look jumbled, the child learns to tolerate a mess. He doesn't have a chance to discover how pleasant order feels.

Also, in a neat-looking room, when a bed is left unmade or clothing is thrown on the floor, it is more obvious—these things look out of place. In a room that looks slightly chaotic to begin with, a few more things strewn here and there will not make much difference.

Whenever possible, choose one central location for all the toys. This area could be a closet, an available wall, or an entire room. Remember, we've been talking in terms of the ideal. Sometimes the design or size of a home makes it impossible to store toys anywhere but the bedrooms. In that case, choose a storage alternative (or a combination of storage alternatives) that will allow you easy maintenance and the look of order.

One home we lived in posed a problem for toy storage. The basement was cold and unfinished so it didn't seem well-suited as a toy depot. And I didn't want to keep the toys in the kids' small bedrooms.

The solution that worked best was this: We stored all the toys in the basement and we let the children bring the toys upstairs to play with. As toys accumulated here and there throughout the day, we put them in a large plastic waste basket that was placed in one of the kid's bedroom closets. Before bed each night, we took the

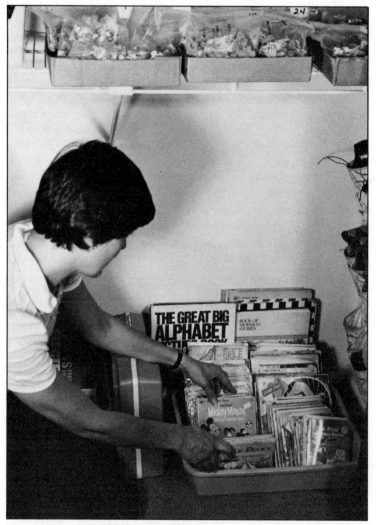

The children's closet showing the four storage alternatives at work for easy access and organization

filled basket downstairs and quickly replaced the toys.

So, try to make the most with what you have to work with. As long as you are using an easy maintenance system that gives the look of order, you're on the right track!

PICKING UP THE PIECES

When our first boy was about two, his dad bought him three Popeye puzzles. The puzzles had about forty pieces, so I put them up until I thought Jimmy was old enough to do them. As he approached three, Jimmy started to ask me for those puzzles. Day after day I told him that the puzzles were too hard. Day after day he persisted. Finally, I got the puzzles down just to prove to him I was right. Needless to say, he sat down and quickly put all three puzzles together.

Since that day, our boys have had a certain fascination for puzzles. I could handle the inlaid puzzles all right. (These puzzles are the kind that come in a frame tray.) They stacked nicely, and being coded, they were never much of a problem, as long as I kept the stack high enough. I must admit that a few times we've had to pick up and put together twenty-five puzzles at the same time. If only I

Inlaid puzzles are coded like this

hadn't trusted a two-year-old not to get into them!

I code the inlaid puzzles for storage as follows: Each puzzle piece is given a letter and the tray where the pieces fit is given the same letter. That way we always know what piece goes with what puzzle. But have you ever seen those giant puzzles? They present quite a different storage problem. What I do with ours is code the puzzle and put all the pieces in a small (but wonderful) plastic food-storage bag. On the bag I mark on masking tape or a self-adhesive label the letter of the puzzle. Then I stand the large puzzle trays in a closet corner. You can either store the bags separately or clamp them to the puzzle tray.

As I said earlier, I could handle the inlaid puzzles. But as our children's skills increased, the puzzles got more complicated. They graduated to jigsaw puzzles (the kind without the tray). No problem, I thought. Those dandy puzzle boxes will be a snap to store.

Well, as Santa Claus says, "Ho, ho, ho!" Little did I realize that those dandy puzzle boxes last long enough for you to do the puzzle about twice. With puzzle boxes and my nerves falling apart at the same rate, I knew I would either have to totally ban puzzles or hope for the manufacturer to recall them. Maybe the Food and Drug Administration would come up with something! I began to get the old toybox terrors again.

Well, American manufacturing came to my rescue with those incredible Ziploc food storage bags. I took all the puzzle boxes and cut out the small sample puzzle pictures from the sides of the boxes. Then I gave each puzzle a number and numbered all the puzzle pieces. (This is easier if you do it when the puzzle is put together. Just turn the completed puzzle upside down and write the number on each piece. This is a job in the beginning, but as we've added new puzzles, it really doesn't take long to process one.) If your puzzle collection is not too large, color coding is an easy alternative. Just run a colored marker over the backs of all the pieces.

I put each puzzle in a separate Ziploc bag. All of our jigsaw puzzles so far (and we have forty) fit into the one-quart size, including the ones with five hundred pieces. Even the puzzles with fairly large pieces fit.

As I described previously, I mark the puzzle number on masking tape or a self-adhesive label and stick it on the bag. Then I stand the bags up in numerical order in a cardboard tray.

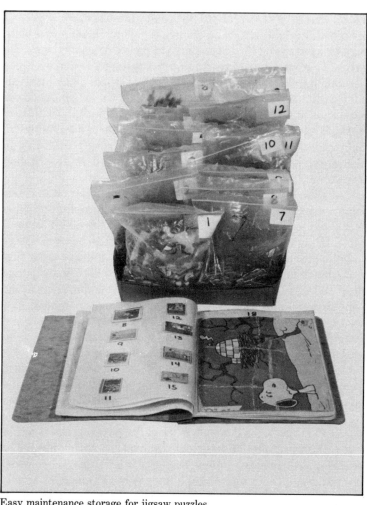

Easy maintenance storage for jigsaw puzzles

I use small pictures of the puzzle to make a catalog. I glue the pictures on paper and write the puzzle number beneath it. The catalog pages are then put in a ring binder. The children look through the catalog and decide which puzzle they want. They see what number it is and go to the puzzle bag with the same number. When I find a puzzle piece on the floor, I pick it up, read the number on it, and pop it into the proper bag!

GAMES PEOPLE PLAY

You may not be aware that game boxes are made by the same people who makes puzzle boxes. Thus, they are equally durable. If you have even one game, chances are you have used tape, staples, rubberbands and cement to hold the box together. Games are expensive and we need to protect our investment, right?

Games have caused me more grief over the years. When I straighten the game closet, I put the largest box on the bottom and stack all the boxes in a neat pile with the smallest box on top. This pyramid storage stystem works very well as long as no one ever uses a game! But, when someone wants Scrabble, they pull it out from the bottom of the stack. Naturally, when it's put away it goes right on top. The result? An upside-down pyramid that soon descends upon the next unsuspecting game player.

A great system for storing games

Once again I was at the mercy of flimsy cardboard boxes. My husband said, sweetly, "You just have to be smarter than the box." Charming man. My frustration led me to a metal parts cabinet, the kind with the plastic drawers. Before I went shopping for this cabinet, however, I analyzed just how much space each game would need. Sorry doesn't have too many accessories, Monopoly and Life have a lot.

So I needed a cabinet with some big drawers, some medium-sized drawers, and some small drawers. I needed a cabinet with enough drawers to hold all our existing game parts, and I wanted to have a few empty drawers to allow for new games that would be added to our collection. I found just what I needed at a discount store. I brought it home and put all the game pieces in the drawers. Each drawer is labeled and some drawers are big enough to hold more than one game. The drawers come with drawer dividers so you can alter the size of the storage spaces within each individual drawer.

You will, of course, run into games that can't be adapted to this idea, like Mr. Mouth, Battleship, and Black Tower. It is convenient, though, to keep the Mr. Mouth chips and the Battleship pegs,

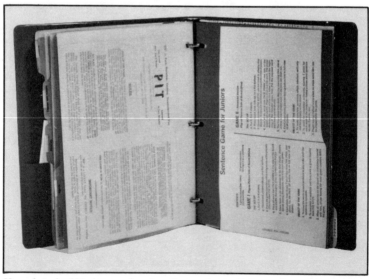

Use a looseleaf binder as a handy reference book of game rules and instructions

etc, in the drawers. It's so much easier to put stray pieces back into the cabinet than it is to wrestle with the boxes. Even though you will have to keep some of the game cartons, you will save a lot of space by using this simple game storage method.

I put all the game directions in a looseleaf notebook in alphabetical order. some game directions are printed on the box lid, thus necessitating photocopying. (And yes, I felt like a fool going into the copy center with a stack of mutilated game box lids under my arm.) A pocket inside the front cover of the same directon notebook holds any game spinners and score pads.

Now when I find a Monopoly house, it easily finds its way home. During a game, if a question about the game rules arises, we simply turn to the direction book. What used to take two shelves now fits nicely on a half shelf. See, we could all live in smaller houses if we got organized. What a great way to fight inflation.

17

Reflections on Collections

The collected mementos of my entire young life would probably fill a dress box. So, I never gave much thought as to how I'd store my children's school papers and childhood keepsakes. I'd simply put all their things into a dress box in chronological order. Then in eighteen years, I'd just hand my child his whole life.

Life has taught me many humbling lessons. What our oldest child brought home the first *day* of kindergarten could easily have filled a dress box. How many blows can one person endure?

Well, I muddled through this sea of papers and watched the rising tide as each of my children went to school I was getting used to the mess when I realized there there was far more than papers collecting. Did you know that kids save used pieces of sandpaper, broken golf tees, and leather covers from old baseballs? What a revelation that was for me! One of our boys even had a dead praying mantis collection.

After coming up for air the third time, I knew it was time for action! Here's what I do now. I have six plastic vegetable bins, one for each child and one for Jim and me. As soon as the kids give me their papers, I put the important ones into their bins. Photographs, birthday cards, and other remembrances are also tossed in.

When the bins are full, I go through them, throwing out some of it, yet keeping a good representation of that child's life. I try to get a cross-section of things so we can always remember what that period of the child's life was really like. I want a true picture; showing likes and dislikes, struggles and strengths.

For example, I recently saved a social studies test that showed a booming score of 14 percent. What was a devastating blow to mother and child will be a riot to a grown adult when he reads that

This type of bin is especially useful for childhood collections

Kansas City is a state and a ghetto is a network of underground subway systems! I have saved Indiana Jones bubblegum cards and pictures of Michael Jackson, Van Halen, and Mr. T, to name a few. I've tried to save everything that says, "This was you." Now, if only I had a picture of a 7-11 store (our home away from home), my collection would be complete.

One of our kids (better known at the note-writing phantom) leaves messages all over the house so we'll know where he is. It isn't uncommon to step out of the shower and see a note taped to the glass door: "Steven is at Benjie's hose." (He doesn't know how to spell *house*, yet.) When waking from a catnap we are likely to find notes taped to our arms, legs, or stomach: "Steven is at Troy's." So we've saved a few of these notes to remind us of this stage in his life. (Yes, when you are organized it is possible to take a nap!)

If you're going to save these valued keepsakes, spend the few extra seconds it takes to label them. If nothing else, indicate the child's name and the date. We have a drawing of that famous story, "Noah's Ark, the Dove and the Alligator"! If I hadn't labeled that alligator, we'd still be wondering what the green thing swimming around the Ark was.

Another time I was going through one of the bins and found a wadded-up, torn piece of paper. I smoothed it out, wondering why I had ever saved such an obvious piece of junk. Then I saw a note I had written: "This was the speech Brian gave when he ran for mayor of the third grade." How grateful I was that I had spent five or ten seconds to write that sentence. I had made a treasure out of something that would have otherwise been trash.

PHOTOGRAPHS

Labeling is also important for photographs. Today you remember the occasion and the names of everyone in the picture. Left unmarked, will that picture mean anything to you twenty years from now?

When the boys were very small I didn't bother to label pictures. I thought surely I would remember all the details about my own kids! I was sadly mistaken. Sometimes when I look at those old photos, the only way I can tell which boy is in the picture is to look at the carpet he's sitting on. (We moved a lot and each boy was a baby in a different house!)

If you're terribly ambitious or if you have a large photograph collection, you might want to start a photo-negative file. I have received many calls and letters from people asking what to do with photo negatives. I didn't have the faintest idea, so I consulted some experts.

The Utah State Historical Society recommends the following catalog system: Number each one of your pictures. Write the number on the back of the picture and write it underneath the picture if it's mounted permanently in an album or book. Then, number each negative to correspond with its printed picture. For example, the picture of Johnny at Sea World would be number one. The negative of the same picture would also be number one.

Number each negative in the margin with India ink. Use a straight-steel dip pen or technical drawing pen, or fountain pen with a fine point since there's not much room in the margin to write on. (Permanent felt marker will work but it is not as permanent as India ink.)

The negatives can be stored in a number of ways. Several numbered negative strips can be placed in an envelope. Number the envelope to correspond with the numbers on the negative (e.g., this envelopes holds negatives numbered one through forty-eight). Also, negative holders called glassine or plastic sleeves are available commercially. They come in a variety of sizes. They can be filed in negative file boxes (also available commercially) or looseleaf notebooks.

There are many products available that will help you organize all your photo supplies. Slide trays provide safe storage and usually come with an index form so you'll know what slides are included in the tray. Slides can be numbered on the frame and the same number put on the indexed tray.

There are many styles and types of photo albums on the market that hold all sizes of photographs. Check a few camera shops and see what organizers are available.

When you're feeling especially energetic, organizing your negatives, slides, and photos ought to keep you out of mischief for awhile!

A LIFE STORY UNFOLDS

Storing these collections needn't be time consuming. Most of us dread tedious hours mounting pictures, filling in baby books, and fussing with scrapbooks. There are easier ways that can be very effective.

For example, every year put each person's collection into a separate manila envelope. Label the envelope with the person's name and the year. Keep the envelopes filed in chronological order and you'll have a life story told with photographs, artwork, school work, and other reminders.

Another method is to put the year and the person's picture on the front of the envelope. Then, keep the envelopes in a looseleaf ring binder.

There are, of course, more complicated systems, if that is your style.. During slow periods throughout the year, I work on life story books for each of us. Each story is illustrated with all the things we store in the bins (photos, samples of school work, copies of important records, pictures of movie stars, etc.)

I type the stories on heavy unruled notebook paper with reinforced margins. This ensures the durability of the book. The material is placed in a ring binder behind a divider with the year typed on the tab. For us, one notebook holds about ten years. (You may have more photos, etc. so your notebook will hold fewer years.) When the boys are ready to leave home they should have two full volumes.

As a guide for writing each life story I let the souvenirs remind me about various events, stages, and interests in that person's life. Also, I ask questions to give me some groundwork. For example:

1. If you could trade places with someone else, who would it be?
2. If you could go anywhere on vacation, where would you like to go?
3. What famous person do you admire most?
4. Who are your favorite movie stars, singers, and sports figures?
5. What is your favorite sport, favorite movie, and favorite song?
6. What do you remember about fifth grade (or whatever)?
7. What would you like to change about yourself?
8. What would you like to change about the world?
9. What do you like to do in your spare time?
10. If you had a million dollars how would you spend it?

Not only are these questions stimulating and fun for the children to answer, they are also effective and revealing for adults. As for the kids, I am always surprised how their answers change from year to year.

ALL THE OTHER STUFF

Now, the paperwork is under control, but there's still the matter of these empty Chapstick cases, "antique" marbles (that they say are worth at least twenty-five dollars each), tiny pieces of ripped paper that contain autographs of people like Marc Wilson, a bicentennial 7-Up bottle, and pieces of satin binding that disintegrated off a security blanket. Personally, I can't stand to see all this stuff and I refuse to clean around it. However, I don't feel that I should inflict my wishes on my children by making them throw everything away. I guess the thought of screaming newspaper headlines haunt me: "MOTHER THROWS OUT CHAPSTICK CASE, SON TURNS TO LIFE OF CRIME."

I don't have the ultimate solution, but I have a few ideas. Children need to have a place for their things. Without a well-defined place for their treasures you will have piles of papers and bottle caps on their dressers and stacks of miscellany on the floor.

A kitty litter pan or dishpan could be used for storage if the problem isn't too severe. Large, covered under-the-bed boxes could be an answer, too. Right now our boys each have a drawer in a nightstand. One of their weekly jobs is to straighten their "junk"

A junk drawer doesn't have to look junky

drawers. There are drawer dividers in these drawers, which further encourage order.

Each of our children also has a large magazine file box to hold their drawings and "important papers." (Important papers are letters to Sheena Easton, pictures of Walter Payton, and Incredible Hulk posters.) The things stored in these boxes are things I am not going to save for their life story books.

These containers will help keep dresser drawers and bedroom floors clutter-free

Oversized things like diplomas, large posters, and perfect attendance certificates can be stored safely if they are rolled up and put inside paper towel tubes or wrapping paper tubes. The labeled tubes can stand upright in a box for easy access.

Here's a great childproof container that has hundreds of uses—9x13-inch cake pans with sliding metal lids. These are especially great for traveling and visiting. They hold coloring books, crayons, books, dolls, and lots of things to keep little hands out of mis-

A cake pan with a sliding metal lid makes a great lap desk

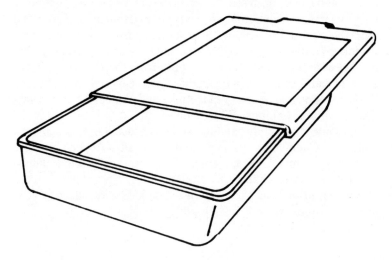

chief. These "lap desks" also make great cake pans during the off season!

Just give each child some kind of container to call his own. An added feature is that these containers are wonderful places to put all those stickers they're always coming up with. Our shoe dishpans were covered with them.

Frankly, I would prefer not to have a box under the bed, stickers on the shoe dishpans, or drawers full of petrified grasshoppers, but I know I have to make concessions. The rule "no stickers on walls, windows, or furniture," is probably realistic, but kids have to have some breathing room, too. I try to remember to give a little here and there.

OLDIES BUT GOODIES

If you're a wife, you're probably thinking: "Great. But my husband still has his eighth-grade P.E. shorts. What do I do with them?" Husbands, on the other hand are saying: "Here are two unopened cases of *Good Housekeeping* magazines she brought with her when we moved from Chicago in 1958."

There's a little child in all of us, I suppose. We still hang on to old letters and cards, high school yearbooks, cheerleading pom-poms, varsity letters, Clark candy bar wrappers (from an old boyfriend with the same name) and leftover nut cups from the twenty-fifth wedding anniversary party. As parents we are continually bombarded with handmade cards and gifts from the children (plaster casts of handprints, paper weights, yarn-covered coat hangers, letter holders, and a variety of pictures and plaques). You can only display so many things. What then?

The same rules apply to adults and children alike. First, discard and sort. Then, box up, label and store all leftovers in a pre-designated, central storage area. (These storage specifics will be covered in a later chapter.)

With an organized plan you and your kids can collect to your heart's content without feeling guilty!

18

Storing the Tools of Your Trade(s)

People who love hobbies can easily have a mess on their hands, and on their floors and tables as well. I know many folks who avoid projects simply because of the general disorder and storage problems that result. What a shame to miss out on the fun of creating for fear of a little chaos and inconvenience. A *little* mayhem never hurt anybody, but using the basic organizing principles we can eliminate a lot of unnecessary clutter.

SEWING AND CRAFTS

Not only can sewing and crafts litter up a house, there are seemingly hundreds of things to store. Have you ever rummaged through a box of fabric trying to find the right piece? And what do you do with miniature novelties or the tips to stylus writing pens? What about seam bindings, hem facings, bias tape, elastic, buttons, trims, ribbons, lace, felt, glue, thread, bobbins, scissors—a person could drown in the debris. It can get complicated. However, order and organization will simpify things. Remember our main premise is to give everything a well-defined place.

STORING FABRIC

Let's start with sewing. The main storage problem I've had with sewing has always been storing fabric and patterns. If you have a lot of fabric to be stored, here's an idea you might like.

Purchase a cardboard covered storage box (the kind you put together yourself) or get a cardboard apple or orange box. Next, you're going to make miniature bolts to wrap your fabric around. Measure the long side of the box and the height of the box. Cut several pieces of corrugated cardboard just one to two inches shorter than the measured length and two inches shorter than the height of the box. (Your "bolts" will be less likely to bend if the corrugation runs vertically rather than horizontally.)

Once that is done, measure and record the widths and lengths of your fabric pieces. When you have made as many bolts as you need, wrap each measured length of fabric around a separate bolt and secure the ends with two straight pins or staples. Now you can flip through your fabric just as you would file folders. To make this even more efficient, here are a couple of things you can do:

Cut a small swatch from each piece of fabric. Secure the swatch with glue or staples to a 3x5-inch index card. Then, on the index card, write the length and width of the fabric and the type of material. Number the index cards and number the fabric bolts to correspond.

The cards can be kept in a file box or in a " magnetic" photo album. Both methods allow for deletions as the fabric is used and additions when new fabric is purchased. The index cards can be categorized by type of fabric.

Instead of the numbering method, you may want to sort your fabric by type or fabric content (e.g., polyester-cotton blends in one box; wool in another). Just be sure to write on the index card which box that particular fabric is in.

You will need one box to hold large, irregularly shaped scraps

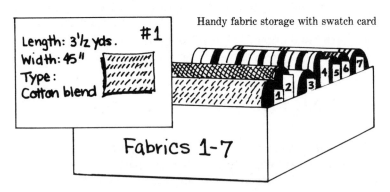

Handy fabric storage with swatch card

Length: 3½ yds. #1
Width: 45"
Type:
Cotton blend

Fabrics 1-7

that cannot be wrapped around a bolt. Cut swatches from these pieces and make up index cards as previously described.

Having all your fabric samples together in a book or file makes it handy to take to a fabric store when you want to choose new fabric to match what you already have at home. The samples are also handy to have when choosing new sewing patterns, and you always know exactly what you have on hand.

The hanging storage alternative can also be used for fabric. Individual pieces of stored material can be folded and hung on clamping pants hangers. Many fabric stores use this method. If you've got plenty of hanging room, this alternative would work very well.

Smaller pieces of material can be folded and placed in plastic food storage bags. Fabric stored in this fashion will be kept clean and the material will stay folded when you're rummaging through a box looking for just the right piece.

STORING PATTERNS

Patterns can be stored efficiently, too. Everyone who sews knows that patterns only fit in the pattern envelope before they are used. Once you've used a pattern, refolding it to fit back into its envelope is nothing short of black magic.

Here are two ways patterns can be efficiently stored. The first is especially effective if you have *a lot* of patterns.

Take the pattern pieces and put them into a 6x9-inch manila envelope. On the envelope write the pattern brand name and number (Simplicity 6184). Take the original pattern envelope and put it into a 6x9 inch looseleaf ring binder. (Punch and reinforce holes on the left hand side of the pattern envelope.) If you prefer, you can open the envelope so the pictures and specification are visible at one glance. Punch and reinforce holes and place the envelopes in a 9x12-inch looseleaf ring binder.

As you place the original pattern envelopes in the binder, you will probably want to arrange them the way they are arranged in the pattern catalogs—according to gender and size. Do not sort the patterns by brand or number. The manila envelopes, however, are filed by brand, numerically.

This is the best method for filing a large number of patterns

When you're all finished, you have your own homemade pattern catalog. Leaf through it until you find the pattern you want. Then, referring to the brand and pattern number on the envelope, go to your filed manila envelopes and pull out the one you want. The pattern catalog is handy to take to a fabric store when you want to buy fabric for one of your patterns.

The second system also works well, and is my favorite—I have a lot of patterns, but not hundreds. Take each pattern envelope and cut it open so that all the pattern specifications are visible. Glue this onto a 9x12-inch manila envelope, and put the pattern pieces inside. Again, arrange the patterns according to size and type. You now have a more durable way to sort your patterns, and the pattern pieces are easier to replace.

Pattern storage in 9x12 manila envelopes

Some sewing experts tell me after they make an outfit they put some fabric scraps and a few extra buttons from the completed project right into the pattern envelope. Then, when a repair is needed, they can find what they need.

NOTIONS, NOVELTIES, AND CRAFT SUPPLIES

My life is over if Ziploc storage bags are ever phased out of production. Here's another way I depend on them. I use a lot of felt and I got tired of hunting through a box full of felt scraps every time I needed a certain color. So I bought a box of the gallon-size ziploc food storage bags. I reinforced the left-hand edge of the bag with masking tape and punched three holes down the side, like notebook paper. I sorted the felt by color and placed each color in a separate bag. Then I put three binder rings through the holes. I now have a nice, neat "book" of felt. The durability of those bags is amazing. I have used my felt book for several years and have not had to replace one bag.

One woman liked this idea so well, she made up a Ziploc "book" and used it to hold Barbie doll outfits—one outfit per page. She says it's the greatest thing ever! Another family uses a Ziploc book to store paper dolls.

This same idea can help you store things such as elastic, seam bindings, ribbons, trims, laces, and embroidery floss using the quart-size Ziploc storage bags.

Ziploc bags can be used for handy storage of felt

I use clear plastic shoe boxes for things such as bias tape, bindings, zippers, buttons, and trims. The boxes stack nicely and, even though they are labeled as to content, I can see at a glance what is in them.

Most of my zippers are recycled, taken from discarded clothing. I measure each zipper, mark the length on masking tape, and put the tape on the bottom edge of the zipper. Each zipper is folded and secured with a rubber band.

The trims, lace, ribbon, and bindings, etc. are wrapped around "mini bolts" I have cut from lightweight cardboard. This way I can flip through the standing "bolts" and choose what I want.

Another see-through shoe box contains my collection of buttons. The buttons are sorted by color and put into quart-size Ziploc bags—red buttons in one bag, brown in another, etc. Button sets or identical buttons are fastened together with hairpins (they're easy to bend). This way I don't have to spend time looking for a set. A plastic shoe box will hold hundreds of buttons!

Skeins of yarn can be stored very decoratively. Open baskets full of yarn add a warm, charming look to a room. Or, hang up a wooden wine rack and store colorful skeins of yarn in each compartment.

Large, round cardboard ice-cream cartons (from Baskin-Robbins or your local ice cream parlor) can be stacked on their sides on a shelf and used as bins for extra skeins. (Did *I* say round?)

Straight knitting needles can be stored in a long aluminum foil box. Browse through a fabric, yarn or craft shop. There are many products available that can help bring order out of anyone's sewing basket (zippered pouches that hold crochet hooks and circular knitting needles, bobbins for embroidery floss, yarn palets for crewel embroidery and needlepoint projects).

Those metal parts cabinets are an organizer's dream. They come in all sizes, with all different-sized drawers. This is a great place for all those little "what do I do with this?" things. Just make sure the drawers are well labeled.

Sewing boxes, cash, tool, or tackle boxes also make great carryalls for sewing or craft projects. You will be able to find a size to fit any need. These same containers are excellent carryalls for all kinds of office supplies.

I hate the get ready and cleanup of craft and sewing projects. I'd much rather leave everything out until the job is completed. However, with lots of little fingers around I can't leave things unattended. So, whenever I can, I use a box or dishpan to hold all my supplies. To get ready, I grab the box. To clean up, I dump everything back in and put it out of sight.

THE WORK ROOM

If you're rebuilding a Model A or sharpening lawn mowers, you probably haven't found this chapter too helpful.

There are ways, though, to keep a garage or workroom from looking like one. (My organized next-door neighbor has a two-car garage that is *so* neat you could easily make a U-turn in it!)

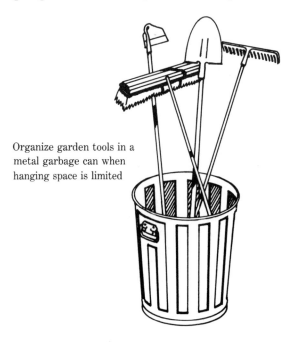

Organize garden tools in a metal garbage can when hanging space is limited

Lawn tools can be hung up on a pegboard or between two closely placed nails. There are also hanging gadgets you can purchase. Check your local hardware and discount stores.

Floor storage is also possible. Put the rakes, hoes, shovels, etc. into a galvanized garbage can and secure the can's handle to a wall to keep it from tipping over. You have given everything a well-confined, well-defined place without using much space.

Dishpans can work wonders in a workroom. Have one for plumbing needs, one for electrical, one for socket wrenches, one for painting and wallpaper accessories, etc. Label the dishpans and keep them on a shelf. Slide out the container and choose what you need. When something needs to be put away, it's just as easy to toss it into a dishpan as it is to put it on the workbench "for now."

Metal parts cabinets with plastic drawers and a variety of other organizers are widely available to hold all your nuts and bolts. Jar lids can be nailed to the underneath side of a shelf and jars full of nails, screws, and washers can be screwed right into the lids.

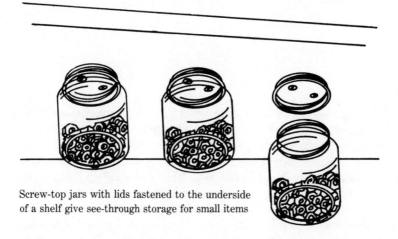

Screw-top jars with lids fastened to the underside of a shelf give see-through storage for small items

Have a special jar or container for screws that you find on the kitchen floor (or wherever). They must have fallen out of something! When you do discover a missing screw, you'll know where to look for it. Also, a houseful of miscellaneous screws won't be scattered here and there or thrown into junk drawers.

Whether the tools of your trade are knitting needles or power saws, you can bring order out of confusion by using the basic organizing principles!

19

The Paper Chase

The biggest threat to a well-ordered home is paper; piles and piles of paper! There are cancelled checks, bank statements, tax records, newspapers, coupons, deeds, loan payment books, sweepstakes notices, directions for cleaning the drapes, service center locations for the Weed Eater, and "The Care and Feeding of a Gerbil." This blizzard of paper could chill the nerves of Dick Butkus (and he's so tough they say he holds his socks up with thumbtacks)!

One woman wrote to tell me, "Sometimes I envy people who have disasters and have everything swept away." I know how she feels. Sometimes I've felt like the paper could sweep *me* away!

A PLACE FOR THE PAPER CHASE

A system for handling paper is an absolute necessity. But, before you can have an effective method, you need to establish a well-defined place in your home in which to conduct the family business.

Ideally, of course, a home office would be located in a separate room with a desk, telephone, filing cabinet, and typewriter. Though the ideal is not always possible, no matter what your circumstances might be, it is possible to have an adequate office center. If a whole room is not available, perhaps there's a small corner tucked away somewhere that would serve the purpose.

First, you will need a surface to write on. This can be a table or a desk. A slab of wood or hollow-core door laid across the top of two filing cabinets can provide you with a perfectly functional home office desk.

Failing that, you can use a portable metal filing case (or cardboard box) to hold your files and a tool or tackle box to hold your office supplies. When you're ready to work, you can carry these two essentials to your kitchen and work on the kitchen table.

A home office also requires a place for storing your files. Filing cabinets (usually two drawers are sufficient), cardboard boxes, expanding files, metal portable filing cases, or under-the-bed boxes are all possiblities.

You will also need some basic supplies:

- Unruled paper and envelopes
- Carbon paper
- Dictionary
- File folders
- Paper clips
- Pencil sharpener
- Pens and pencils
- Rubber bands
- Ruler
- Scissors
- Cellophane tape
- Stamps
- Your calendar or complete planning notebook

A typewriter, telephone, and a calculator would be very convenient, but they are not necessary.

The main thing is to know where everything is. Have all your supplies close to your files and writing surface so you won't have to chase back and forth looking for something you need.

ORGANIZING A HOME FILING SYSTEM

Now, let's put our home office center to use. You should keep three home files (in addition to a safe deposit box at your local bank). These three files are:

1. Active File
2. Dead File
3. Permanent Reference File

The *active* file contains material of specific and current interest to the family. These are the papers that keep the family running smoothly (so the water isn't turned off, the IRS is happy, and you can find the manual for the air conditioner when it goes on the blink).

The *dead* file contains tax working papers (bill receipts, bank statements, cancelled checks) over three years old.

The *permanent reference* file is for articles, poems, stories, newspaper clippings, craft patterns, music, etc. This file is for things you want to keep indefinitely to refer to and enjoy. The permanent reference is discussed in detail in the chapter entitled "The Finishing Touch."

Your safe deposit box should contain the following documents:

1. Birth certificates
2. Citizenship papers
3. Marriage certificates
4. Adoption papers
5. Divorce decrees
6. Wills
7. Death certificates
8. Deeds
9. Titles to automobiles
10. Household inventory
11. Veteran's papers
12. Bonds and stock certificates
13. Important contracts (papers that serve as proof of ownership, leases, patents, copyrights, etc.)

WANTED: DEAD OR ALIVE!

In this section, I will describe how I use my active and dead files to manage all the paperwork that comes into our home.

In the front of my active file I have fifteen file folders: *financial, to do, to file,* and one for each month of the year.

Behind these are folders with various subject headings. Some ideas are:

Employment records (résumés, letters of recommendation, previous employers, health benefit information), current health benefit information, credit card information, insurance policies, wills (copies), health records, education information (schools attended, degrees, awards, activities, transcripts), safe deposit box inventory (and extra key), record club, car information, services (lawn care, plumber, paper hanger, electrician, building contractor), amusement parks (tickets leftover from Disneyland), scouting information, restaurants (menus for take-out and other information), store or product information, and whatever is of interest to you.

In back of the active file, I have an A-to-Z expanding file that holds instruction booklets, warranties (the receipts for the products are stapled right to the warranty), appliance manuals, and other product information, etc.

The stereo booklet is filed under S, the refrigerator manual is filed under R, how to clean the drapes is filed under D and so on. These things are used so seldom they do not require more detailed filing.

Here's how the system works:

The financial folder holds anything relating to money: all the unpaid bills, current bank statement and cancelled checks, receipts for any charged items, payment and loan booklets, etc. A subscription renewal notice would go into this folder because a payment has to be made.

The to-do folder holds letters that you need to answer, calls and appointments you need to make. A wedding invitation would go into this folder. You need to write the date and address of the wedding on your calendar. You need to RSVP and buy a gift. Once all these things are done, discard the invitation, unless pertinent information is included.

To file is exactly that. For simplicity, file things under the broadest possible subject. Use the active file list for possible categories.

Also through the mail (and elsewhere) you receive things of interest to other people in the family: personal letters, information about your son's upcoming football camp, notice of a ground beef sale from the butcher, *Sports Illustrated*, etc.

Have one spot designated to put this incoming mail so everyone in the family always knows where to look for it. If you want to keep it out of sight, designate a drawer (be careful, here), file folder, or basket to hold this miscellaneous material. As soon as possible, get these things into the mainstream of the paper handling process. (When a decision about football camp is reached, schedule it in your calendar, send in the registration form, etc.)

Schedule an hour or so each week to handle paper. As soon as the mail arrives, decide what to keep and what to discard. Do not keep anything that is not currently of interest to someone in your family, even if it might come in handy someday! (Ask yourself, "What will happen if I throw this away?")

Quickly put each item into its proper folder. If something needs to be taken care of before your next office session, note it in your calendar so it won't be forgotten.

The financial folder is handled in a very simple manner. After you have paid a bill, retain the stub for your records and place it in the current month's folder. For example, you would put January statements in the January folder, and so on. After you have reconciled your January bank statement, put it in the January folder.

What could be easier? So many times we make our systems so complicated and precise they seem to invite piling up and procrastination. I've had people tell me, "I really like my system. It's different from yours, but I really like it. I haven't had time to get to it lately, but when it's working, I sure like it!" If your system is not simple enough to keep up with, you've made it too complicated.

You don't need to have a folder for every company you do business with and you don't need to sort out tax information every month (unless you really want to).

Records need to be reviewed at least once a year to discard things you no longer need. January is a good month for this job because tax time is just around the corner.

During January have a tax session to sort out and categorize your tax deductions. Then, discard the following:

1. Salary statements (after you check them against your W-2 form)

2. Cancelled checks for cash or nondeductible items. (NOTE: if you have cancelled checks for large purchases you may want to keep them for insurance purposes.)
3. Expired warranties
4. Expired coupons
5. Other things no longer needed

After the tax return is completed, I put the following into a large manila envelope:

1. Paid bill receipts
2. Bank statements
3. Cancelled checks
4. Other tax working papers

The envelope is dated (Year Ending) and filed in back of the active file. When the envelope is three years old, I take it out and move it to the dead file.

The dead file is seldom used and can be stored in your storage area or some other out-of-the-way place.

Shortly after the first of the year, then, your monthly financial folders should be empty and ready to use for another year. The rest of your active file should be current and in continual use.

HOUSEHOLD INVENTORY

If you've ever been the victim of a fire or burglary, then you already know the value of having a household inventory. The inventory shows what you possess and how much it is worth. An inventory may also show that you do not have adequate insurance to cover the value of your possessions.

A simple way to make an inventory is to use a tape recorder. As you enter each room in your house (don't forget the attic, basement, and garage), start at a certain point and move around the room in a circle. Speak into the microphone and say exactly what the object is, how much it cost when it was purchased and how much it would cost to replace it. Be sure to include serial numbers, model numbers, brand names, dealer's name, and description of the article. (Many people take pictures of their possessions, thus eliminating some of the description process. Expensive items such as silver, gold and jewely require closeup photographs.) Check with your insurance agent for your company's exact requirements. If you wish, you can transcribe your taped recording onto paper.

Update your inventory every six months by adding new purchases, or make deletions and indicate new replacement costs (if possible). You may want to type two copies of your tape recording, or perhaps you will choose to write your inventory initially. Whatever method you use, an inventory may be very useful to you. Keep one copy of it in your safe deposit box.

Finally, make a record of where all your important papers are located. A looseleaf binder (filed in your active file) is a good place for this information.

What to include:

1. List of all bank accounts
2. Where safe deposit box is located
3. All family members' social security numbers
4. Insurance policy numbers and agents' names
5. Copy of household inventory
6. Record of household improvements

This system isn't necessary, but some type of system is!

Whatever method you use, make sure that someone else in your family knows and understands it.

20

The Finishing Touch—Your Permanent File

I love to save useful bits of information: decorating tips, information on drug and alcohol abuse, needlework and craft patterns, holiday ideas and activities, exercises and physical fitness information, sheet music, pictures for visual teaching aids and school reports—I could go on forever! I also love to be able to find one of these aids when I want it. This chapter is devoted to the method I use to file things I want to keep and refer to indefinitely.

If I were the Surgeon General, I would put a warning right here before going any further! WARNING: *This filing system is not for everyone*. It is ambitious and requires some paperwork. It *is* for the person who, like me, loves to collect things and needs to refer to them often.

If you choose to skip this chapter (which is perfectly okay), you can still save clippings, ideas, and articles. Just put your assorted collection into file folders labeled by subject, then file them alphabetically. For example: all photography articles are put into a folder labeled photography. When a new article on photography is clipped out, pop it into the photography folder. This is the beginning of your permanent file (not to be confused with the active and dead files discussed in the previous chapter).

THE NUMERICAL FILING SYSTEM

As a teenager, my good mother taught me the value of establishing a collection of articles and pictures. One of my favorite hobbies was working on my files, arranging and categorizing them by subject. However, as I grew older, I collected more and more things and my subject file grew more complicated. Some things had more than one subject. Some things, such as humorous articles and certain pictures, seemed to have no specific subject. I wanted a better, more efficient system.

The system I use now is a simple numerical system. This system is one of the many different methods developed for office use, but it works extremely well at home.

Imagine for a minute that you had a large book in your home library. Suppose this book contained many different subjects. To find exactly what you wanted, you would look in the index, wouldn't you? The index would tell you on what page the needed information was located.

Basically, this is what you are going to do—set up an index to lead you to anything in your file. Each file entry will be numbered (like the pages of a book), and the index will tell you on what page your needed information is located. When this file system is functioning efficiently, it can lead you to anything in your home.

I have a crocheted North Pole scene that I've made for Christmas. Each year, I try to add one or two pieces to it. (The first year I made Santa, the next year, Rudolph, and so on.) One day I wanted a pattern for a crocheted polar bear I had seen in a craft magazine. I went to my file and in less than a minute, I had the pattern in my hands.

One day our oldest son came home from school and said he needed to make a poster for science about drug abuse. He didn't know what to do or where to begin. I took him down to the file and in less than a minute he had a fist full of information! (He got an A on his poster, too.)

This filing system can work well for you too. How many times have you perched yourself behind a stack of magazines looking for that article you know you saw somewhere. If only you could remember where you saw it. Well, this system will change all that. All it takes is a little time and a few inexpensive supplies.

You will need to get several index cards, either 3x5 or 4x6. I use the 4x6 size. You will also need some alphabetical guides (the same size as your index cards) and a small file box to put them in. Together, these supplies will make up the index to your file. It will function just as a book index functions.

You will also need some file folders. I use letter size, but legal size could also be used. You will need approximately one folder for every twenty-five things you have to file. Also, you will need to have a container to hold these folders. A filing cabinet is not necessary; cardboard boxes, cardboard file drawers, or portable metal filing cases can work just as well.

Once you have your supplies, you're ready to start. With many filing systems, it is necessary to sort or alphabetize the information to be filed. Not so with this method. You can start with a random pile of things, discarding unnecessary items as you file.

Just follow these simple steps:

1. Take a file folder and put the numerals 1 through 25 on the tab. (A folder can hold about twenty-five things without crowding.) Mark your other file folders in groups of twenty-five; i.e., 26-50; 51-75; etc.

2. Pick up the first article to be filed. Put the number 1 in the upper or lower right-hand corner. (Whichever you choose, make sure you mark all the rest of the articles to be filed in the same corner.) Just for the sake of example, let's say that the first thing you want to file is an article on ways to welcome a new neighbor:

When visiting a newcomer to your neighborhood, bring a brown paper bag that contains this message and four earthly symbols.

"Welcome to your new home. It is an ancient tradition that upon moving into a new home a family should be made welcome with these four earthly symbols: a sponge that the house may always be clean, a loaf of bread that there may always be food upon the table, sugar that there may be sweetness abounding, and salt that there may be some spice in living."

3. On an index card, write *Neighbors* on the top line. Under the heading put the number 1. Then briefly describe the article in a way that will help you remember it.

If the title of the article or the name of the author means anything to you, make out index cards with the author or the article title on them, such as, "Hi, Neighbor" or Clarke, Judith (I only do this when I have a good reason to believe I'll never forget the author's name or the title of the article.)

Let's pretend that this article about welcoming new neighbors also discussed how children can participate in the welcoming process. Then you would want to make up another index card with the heading Children. On each of these index cards briefly describe the article. Just be sure that you make up index cards for every subject that the article covers.

Neighbors

1. Article describing how to welcome new neighbors with bread, salt, sponge, sugar.

---

4. Put the article in the 1-25 folder.

5. File the index cards alphabetically in the file box. Now, you are probably thinking that this is a lot of work. It is! But I know from experience that time well invested is future time saved. Sometimes you have to spend time to save time.

As you are filing, keep the following things in mind. Most of the time, you will have to make out more than one card for each item that you file. For example, if you want to file a pattern for a stuffed Snoopy, you may want index headings like *Snoopy*, *toys*, *dog*. Just make out your index cards in your own words using headings that will make it easy for you to find what you want. When you read through an article, make an index card for every subject it covers (or at least the subjects you are interested in).

Also, there will be several entries listed on one card. When you come across another article about neighbors, you will list it under the first entry on your neighbor card, and so forth. I write on the back of my index cards when the front is filled.

Now, when you come across something in a magazine or book that you can't tear out, here's what you do: Instead of giving the article (or whatever) a file number, simply write on the index card where it can be located, by author, title, publication information, and page number.

MAKE IT WORK FOR YOU

Once you've gotten a firm grip on the basic procedure, you'll want to make the file system work for you. Let me describe how I adapted the systems to my own likes and interests.

First, I only group things together that will always be used together. For example, *Halloween, Thanksgiving,* etc.; *interior decorating ideas; party invitations,* and *announcements* (I save especially clever announcements and invitations I receive just for ideas); *exercises, information on drug abuse*—to name a few. When things are grouped together I give everything in that group the same number.

Occasionally, I have things that I sometimes want all together and sometimes I just want a particular thing from that group. For example, I have a collection of children's stories. I put all the stories in a looseleaf binder and gave the binder a number. This binder is filed in numerical order along with my file folders. Then each page in the book is numbered. Each story is filed as a separate article such as:

Manners
384   Peter Learns How To Have Good Manners page 31.

This way, if I just want to sit down with a book of stories, I go to my file and get the binder. However, if I want a story about manners, I look in my index under *manners* and I'll see on my manners card that I have children's stories regarding manners. So, I can enjoy the best of both—grouped system, or single.

Remember, this is just the way I do it. You may want to change some areas, or add items to fit your particular needs. Just make the system work for you.

When filling out your cards you may want to set up a code for yourself such as: S—Subject, P—Pictures, FB—Flannelboard characters or flannelboard story, M—Music, NWC—Needlework and crafts. These abbreviations will help eliminate writing the words over and over.

STORING THE FILES

A filing cabinet is ideal if you have enough to fill it! Otherwise there are several alternatives we have already discussed.

Because my hoard is large, I have a filing cabinet. Here's how I use it.

In the top drawer I have filed in alphabetical order unruled paper, carbon paper, construction paper, file folders, graph paper, manila envelopes, ruled paper, etc. Each particular group is placed in its own file folder behind a labeled, tabbed divider.

Then, I have one whole file drawer full of pictures I use for visual aids, one drawer on assorted subject matter (things I want to keep and refer to indefinitely), and one drawer of needlework and craft patterns. Because I have a large collection, I have chosen to keep these categories separate, although it is not necessary. The index cards are filed in groups, too. Pictures are filed together on blue index cards, needlework and crafts are filed together on pink index cards, and subject information is filed together on white index cards. This eliminates confusion when I'm refiling an index card.

(I especially love having all my craft patterns together. It's just like a giant craft book complete with an index!)

KEEPING ON TRACK

I have a folder in the front of my subject drawer that holds the following:

1. An index card on which is written the next available number in each category. This will prevent you from going through your files trying to see what number you are on, for example:

NWC   142 (Free 87)
Subject   397 (Free 71)
Pictures   691 (Free 14)

The next item filed in my subject file will be given the number 397. The next craft pattern I file will be numbered 142, and so on.

When you set up your files, you are likely to be interrupted. This will sometimes cause you to skip a number here and there. After you've completed your file, go through the filed items and check to see if you've used every number. If you find you've skipped one or two, write it down as a free number. Then, when you have a new article to file, you can use your free numbers first and fill in the gaps.

2. Items to be filed.

3. Check-out sheets. If anyone wants to borrow an item, be sure to write down the number and description, the date, and person borrowing. Let me warn you—once you get your system going, you will receive many requests from well-meaning friends and relatives. I have just started to keep photocopies of things people want to borrow. I have learned the hard way that you don't always get back the things you lend out, even if you keep track of who has borrowed from you. Most of the time people will absolutely swear that they gave it back!

This system is great for music. My sheet music is numbered and index cards are filed alphabetically by the song title. Music is also grouped together. Index cards could also be made up by composer and lead you to a page in a book or a single piece of music.

Here's another way this system can help—I have a permanent section in my calendar entitled *Thoughts*. Whenever I read, I keep my calendar nearby to jot down motivating thoughts and ideas. If I'm attending a meeting or a class, I bring my book and write down quotes, thoughts, and anything that motivates me. Each entry is numbered so I can file its location in my card file.

So, if I want a particular item in my book of thoughts, I use my card file as an index to my book. Rereading my book of thoughts is a real source of self-motivation.

Success

"Thoughts" No. 126

DON'T STOP NOW

Remember, the index card file can tell you where anything in your house is kept or stored. It's up to you. However you use your files to help you remember where the canteen is kept, or where a favorite poem is filed, you can save a lot of time.

You can even file a list of things you always take camping or vacationing. Every year at vacation time I sit down and write basically the same list that I've written every year before. Why waste the time when my file can do the listmaking for me? Of course, there are usually a few variables, but a basic permanent list could save hours of time and would eliminate the nagging thought, "I wonder what I've forgotten."

Use your imagination and expand on this idea. Could you use a list of party preparations? Look through your lists and notice which ones keep recurring. Every time you make a new list ask yourself if you'll ever be able to use the same list in the future.

Remember, this numerical system is totally optional. It is good for those who don't mind paperwork. It is an efficient system for a person who has a large collection of information and refers to it often.

If you do not fall into this category, breathe a sigh of relief! You do not want or need such a system.

For those who do feel a need for a fast, effective method, this is by far the best! It's a good project to do while watching TV. It is easy to set up and maintain using small pieces of time.

Good luck and start as soon as you can. The time you waste may be your own! What a relief to save whatever you want and find it when you need it!

21

The Story on Storage

We're nearing the end of our journey. We've planned and uncluttered, filed, and fed. If you've done your job well, you should have a lot of things needing to be stored. Only the real necessities should be taking up precious space in your drawers and shelves. Now, what to do with all the leftovers?

First, let's make a last-ditch effort to eliminate as much as possible. Before you store anything, make sure you really need it. There's no sense storing a flash attachment from an old, discarded camera, lids to broken casserole dishes, or two books left from your set of 1947 encyclopedias. Once again, think through your belongings. Do you really need the things you are planning to store.

Before putting anything into storage ask yourself, "What would happen if I got rid of this?" If the answer is, "Nothing," that should tell you something. Also, ask yourself "How hard would it be to replace this object should I decide to get rid of it?" Using these two questions as guidelines will help you be more objective.

Once you're ready, you need a program that will make it quick and easy to find and use the things you've stored. Here's what I do:

Most of my storage items are kept in covered cardboard apple or orange boxes. I have found that if I cut the lids down (so they are only four or five inches deep) the boxes are much easier to open. You may also want to cut "handle" holes in the side of the boxes. Accessibility is the key to an efficient storage system.

Once you have a supply of boxes, sort your things into groups. The groupings I use are: *Adult*—adult clothing, including maternity clothing: *Baby*—baby clothing through size two and baby equipment; *Children*—children's clothing (size three and over) and children's shoes; *Decorations*—all holiday decorations (if you have a lot of decorations, rather than grouping decorations into one large categroy, you may prefer to break them down into individual groupings, such as CH—Christmas, HA—Halloween, E—Easter, V—Valentines, T—Thanksgiving); *Furnishings*—throw rugs, bedspreads, blankets, curtains, drapes, etc.; *Household*—dishes, gadgets, small appliances, pans.

After the boxes are packed and labeled, code your boxes with permanent marker. The first box of adult clothing is marked A-1. The second is marked A-2 and so on. Using this method, I use the following code: A-adult, B-baby, C-children, D-decorations, F-furnishings, H-household.

Perhaps you will have more or different categories. I simply use the first letter of each category as the code letter. That way, it's easy to remember.

Now let me explain why I code at all. Let's say I want the cornucopia for a centerpiece. Since I use it as a Thanksgiving decoration I know it's going to be in a box labeled D for *decorations*. I go out to my shelves where all the boxes are stored and go right to the D boxes. The list of contents on each box quickly tells me which D box contains the cornucopia.

Cornucopia
Box D·2

Also, if you choose to be so organized, you can make an index card for each of your storage items (or groups of storage items). Another method is to make a list wherein all your storage items and their locations are listed. Then, when you want something, check your list (or index card) and see where it is stored.

I feel, however, that it's easier to go directly to your storage area, read your coded boxes and get what you want immediately. This method eliminates extra time spent looking in a card file or checking through a list. Remember, too, the extra time involved when you have to add or delete entries on lists and card files. It's much easier to cross off or add something to the side of a box.

Then again, if you have ten boxes in one group, maybe it would be easier to check a card file than read the contents of ten boxes. You decide and choose the system that will best suit your storage needs.

Clothing storage is usually a problem, especially where children's apparel is concerned. The longer clothes are stored, the worse they look, so be selective about the things you save. Don't accept hand-me-downs from others if you don't need them.

Perhaps you've had the experience of going through a storage box only to find a great article of clothing you forgot about; now, it's too small for the child! One idea that can help is to have two storage boxes for each child (whenever practical). One box can hold out-of-season clothes, and one can hold clothes to grow into. Another method is to sort things by season, sex, and size.

With inexpensive molding (nailed into the studs of all three sides of the wall) and particle board, you can build an extra shelf above the installed closet shelf. Use the shelf to store the out-of-season and grow-into boxes right in the child's room. This will create easy storage access using what would otherwise be wasted space.

One-motion storage is extremely important to any storage program. Things that are too big to be stored in boxes should be kept in clear plastic bags (when necessary) so they are in full view. Having your storage shelves too wide will force you to store things one in front of the other, thus defeating your one-motion storage goal.

If boxes are hard to get to or difficult to open, you'll probably start piling things up "for now" with plans to put them into storage boxes later.

Make your system easy to use and easy to get to. It'll cut down on procrastination. Simplify things, make them convenient, and you will be more likely to follow through with your program.

PART THREE

Getting Started

22

How to Organize Another Person

Who is this paragon of virtue, this man of steel, who is able to bend wire in his bare hands (and throw the scraps into the junk drawer).

This man of might, disguised as a husband, is more powerful than a locomotive (when he's hauling things *home* from the dump); able to leap tall piles of dirty clothes in a single bound (when he's heading for the shop); and faster than a speeding bullet (when it's time for a ballgame).

The question I am asked over and over is, "How can I organize my husband?" First, you must realize that is a difficult question. There are men out there who still have the hubcaps from their first car!

Men aren't the only offenders, though. Many men have complained to me about all the junk their wives have hoarded. One man called to say, "For years my wife blamed everything on the kids. Now the kids are gone and the house is still a wreck. She saves *everything*."

One woman always bragged that it didn't make any difference to her husband how the house looked. All the confusion didn't bother him one little bit! One evening this woman gathered her family around her and passed out a sheet of paper to each one. She innocently asked everyone to list the goals they had for themselves and for the family. When the papers were passed back, she was surprised by her husband's responses. Everything on his list had to do with bringing more order, organization, and peace into their home!

I know of one man who solved his junk accumulation problem by building a storage area in the rafters over his garage. That, he thought, would pacify his wife. It did, for awhile, until the roof over the garage began to give way. His wife was almost delighted thinking now he would surely have to dispose of his "collection."

Never fear, this Metropolis Marvel outwitted his wife! Armed with several two-by-fours he propped up the roof and (just in the knick of time) saved his treasures from obliteration.

Obviously, some people are resourceful (and stubborn) little devils who are bound and determined to collect and stash their trash. In many cases it does cause frustration and disharmony at home.

This is the only area where I can't guarantee success, but I know four simple rules that will help.

RULE NUMBER ONE:
SET AN EXAMPLE

Unfortunately, one of the first rules of organization is: You cannot organize another person. You can, however, set a good example. Sometimes, when people begin to see the amounts of time and money saved through an organizational program, they begin to follow suit. Patience is the major factor here.

Chances are when you undertake an organizational project everyone in the family is going to think you're going through a stage that will soon pass. More than likely, they will ignore any attempts on your part to get things into shape. It's only when you hang in there and your efforts pass the test of time that they will realize you mean business.

RULE NUMBER TWO:
TALK IT OVER

Tell your spouse once that it is important to you to have a smoothly running system. Saying it more than once constitutes nagging and will cause further discord.

One wife complained that her husband always put kitchen utensils away in the wrong place. One day she told him that she had designated certain places for each gadget. She further explained to him that the things were there for a reason. As soon as he saw the logic behind her system, he cooperated. So tell your mate once and see what happens.

Tell the children what you're doing. Ask for their ideas. They love to feel that they're part of things, and they'll be more willing to cooperate.

After planting his garden, our neighbor was worried about the rowdy little boy who lived next door to him. He was afraid the boy would tromp through the plants and destroy the crops. This man decided to make the child a part of the project. "Freddy," he said, "I've just planted my garden. I'm afraid that the neighbor children will run through it and ruin it. Will you help me guard these plants?" Freddy rose to the occasion and watched those plants like a professional security guard.

So, draw the kids into the project by asking for their help and ideas.

Try a tradeoff. Tell him if he'll hang up his clothes, you'll take out the garbage. Tell her you'll change diapers if she'll weed the garden. Discuss which chores are most distasteful to each of you, and see if a tradeoff is possible. This can work with children, too!

Be understanding. There are probaby certain things that you do that are irritating. Giving and taking is what a good relationship is all about. What may seem like a worthless trinket may be as valuable to your spouse as the car is to you.

RULE NUMBER THREE: MAKE IT CONVENIENT

Convenience is extremely important when trying to unclutter another person. If you are using the principle of giving things a well-defined, well-confined place, you have already brought much convenience into your home.

The family has to relearn where things belong and they won't always cooperate. But if you persist and keep returning things to their well-defined places, eventually the family will join forces with you. They will have a clear vision in their minds where things belong, rather than a vague idea.

Our youngest son often plays Superman or Batman and needs to wear a cape. He goes into the bathroom and selects just the right towel. Then he gets a safety pin to secure his costume. Every time he wants a safety pin, he knows exactly where to get one. They are always where they are supposed to be. When he is finished playing superhero and I ask him to put the safety pin back, he knows *exactly* where it belongs.

Be sure family members see that your improvements are saving time, energy, and sometimes money.

When our children were younger, each boy had a dishpan on the floor of his closet to hold his shoes. Their shoes were small, so even though they had several different pairs (Sunday shoes, play shoes, and slippers), they all fit nicely into the dishpan. We seldom had to look for shoes because they had a well-defined, convenient place.

If someone is constantly dropping clothes where they were taken off, ask that person if they'll at least put them all in the same corner or on the same chair. Whoever picks up the mess will have it all in one place instead of *every* place.

Put a basket on top of a dresser or on the refrigerator (or wherever) to hold business cards, keys, change, and miscellaneous tidbits that come home in pockets or purses. Instead of having this stuff thrown on the table, it can be out of sight in a decorative basket. (To avoid turning this catch-all into a "junk drawer," clean it out every few days.)

If your collector isn't using certain things and still refuses to get rid of them, box them up and store these boxes in a storage area. Put the person's name and the date on the box. The offender will have the security of knowing the belongings are safe and close at hand. Chances are that in six years, when they see the date on the box, they will see the folly of their ways and give some things away. (My sister has several boxes in her basement: Tom's box No. 1, Tom's box No. 2, Tom's box No. 3 . . .)

If family members have to go upstairs (or downstairs) to put the scissors away, then they probably won't. They'll just stick the scissors in a handy spot and you'll have to look for them the next time you want them.

Think of the things you lose or misplace most often and ask youself these questions:

1. Where is this item mostly used?
2. Do I keep this in a convenient place?
3. Does it have a well-defined place?

4. Do I need more than one? (Example: one pair of scissors upstairs and one downstairs.)

People often ask me why the glue and scissors are always where they are supposed to be in my house. One reason is that we usually use glue in two rooms; the kitchen and a downstairs room next to the family room. So I keep two sets of these things, one set in each room. When the glue is used in the kitchen, it stays in the kitchen, even though it may not be put back into the drawer where it belongs. (To be honest, my kids don't put things away any better than anyone else's kids do.)

Try to be persistent. When you find a safety pin, put it where it belongs. When you find a pencil, put it away. Soon everyone will see the rewards of order—no more looking and searching. Everything will be found when it's needed. Impatience and irritation will not be as frequently felt or expressed! Gradually they'll come to realize that your improvements are saving time, energy, and money. Convenience will teach family members that order gives much more pleasure than disorder.

RULE NUMBER FOUR: PRAISE

As a motivator, nothing works like sincere praise. When things are messed up after all your hard work, refrain from criticism. That will only cause more resistance. A good measure of praise for jobs well done will get much better results.

One night after dinner our oldest boy picked up his dishes and brought them over to the sink. After picking myself up from a dead faint, I complimented him on his thoughtfulness. But I didn't stop there. I told everyone that I had a boy who brought his dishes to the sink after eating.

One evening, his teacher called me. "Mrs. Schofield," she said, "we're celebrating Jimmy's birthday tomorrow. Can you tell me a few things about him—his favorite color, favorite food, a good habit?" You can be sure I told her his good habit and she announced it to his whole class the next day. Even though that was several years ago, Jimmy is still bringing his dishes to the sink. He has to live up to his reputation.

Don't forget appreciation and praise works for adults, too.

If you do find it necessary to correct or criticize, try the "sandwich" principle. Simply stated, that is a bad remark sandwiched between two good remarks. Sometimes it's been so bad around here I've had to say, "The ceiling in here looks great! You really need to get rid of this junk on the floor, though. I'm happy to see one of your shoes in the shoebag." Anyway, I'm sure you get the idea. Just find two good points even if you have to stretch it a bit, and sandwich a bad one in between.

Try these four simple rules. I can't promise anything, but I'm sure you'll at least see an improvement.

There's one more problem we haven't covered—the problem of undoing a hard day's work.

After giving a lunch-and-learn lecture at the Internal Revenue Service a member of the audience asked me: "I know I can go home and do all of this. I also know that in one week, I'll have to do the whole thing over. What can I do?"

Another question that often arises is, "What do you do when you've spent all day cleaning and the kids come home and undo everything in five minutes?" In the interest of space, I will try to condense my remarks! I believe there are entire books written on this subject.

I know the frustrations that are born out of this situation, because I have felt them also. I feel strongly, though, that herein lies the greatest reason in the world to get organized.

If you are only a surface cleaner, then the children really are undoing all your hard work. It is difficult and time consuming to clean and maintain order when things under the surface are not in tiptop shape. When the kids undo, you really are at point zero—again! No wonder we suffer from frustration and depression.

Imagine for a minute that you live in a home that is clutter free. Everything in the home has a well-defined, well-confined place. Cleaning an already orderly home is twice as fast and half as fatiguing. The kids come home from school, drop their coats and boots in the corner, throw their papers and books on the counter, grab a snack, spill the milk, drop crumbs on the floor and so on. Sure, the surface is getting messed up, but underneath it all there is still peace and order. Cupboards, closets, and drawers are still neat and tidy. Things can still be found and put away quickly. In a home such as this, bringing the surface under control is not really a big deal.

Before the situation is really out of control, start controlling it. Protect your investment by spending a few minutes to regain a semblance of order. If you delegate, follow through. If you do it yourself, don't complain.

Remember, how long does it really take to straighten up an organized, orderly home? Not long at all! Believe me, the road to getting organized is the road to better mental health.

Whatever course of action you take, don't let your desire for order ruin your marriage or your family life. Next time you are faced with another mess, step back, take a deep breath, and say to yourself, "This is the signature of someone I love!"

23

Interruptions—the Hidden Destroyers

Housework is more subject to interruptions than any other field of human endeavor! It is any wonder we sometimes want to get away from it all? How we long to lock the world out and bask in the sunshine of uninterrupted time.

While this is a delightful fantasy, we all need to realize that a certain number of interruptions are to be expected. However, many interruptions are not necessary and can be skillfully eliminated. We need to learn how to work in spite of them. One important principle I still struggle with is this: Don't let an imperfect situation be an excuse to do nothing. Interruptions will never go away, so don't wait for them to disappear before you start something.

What are the hidden interruptions in your life? One easy way to determine what (or who) the time-destroyers are is to spend a few minutes at the end of the day thinking about where your time went. Jot down the little irritations and interruptions that obstructed your progress. Quickly note how your time was spent. After several days you may notice a trend. What problems keep recurring?

You may feel that spending a few minutes a day analyzing your time expenditure is asking a little much. However, if you are feeling unfulfilled and frustrated, it is necessary for you to do this. The result of getting control over your time will be greater freedom! You can spend all day putting out fires or you can catch the guy with the matches—the choice is yours.

Another thing you can try is to jot down each interruption as it occurs; noting who the interrupter was, when it happened and what was needed. This makes for a slightly chopped-up day, but it is a very effective short-term exercise. When done for four or five days, it will give you a clear indication of what is happening to your time and who the chief offender is.

You may discover that many of your interruptions are caused by someone not being able to find something. Perhaps there is not an adequate laundry routine and lack of the desired clothing is causing problems. Maybe meals are not well planned and prepared, causing constant eating and unscheduled trips to the store. Be honest with yourself and identify those time robbers. Knowing the cause of your problems will lead to the solutions.

Many times we cause our own problems. If you're really frustrated with your lack of time and feel as if you never get anything accomplished, you need to take more drastic measures. I don't usually recommend this, because most people won't follow through with it. However, it is a very revealing project that can put you on track.

The method is simple. Keep a log of your entire day in fifteen-minute increments. Do this consistently for four or five days and you will learn a lot about yourself and your family.

After doing this activity myself, I thought it was kind of fun and it opened my eyes. I always hated changing sheets on the bed. But after keeping this time chart, I discovered it only took two or three minutes for this job. Now, I don't mind changing sheets at all.

This chart will tell you how much time you spend sleeping, eating, reading, watching TV, talking on the phone and how long it takes to clean the bathroom. You will have a bird's-eye view of where your time goes. You may even surprise yourself and see that you are accomplishing a great deal more than you thought. The chart will also tell you if you're too busy and need to say no more often. You may see a need for more delegation. There are many things to be done, but where is is written that YOU have to do them all?

Your attitude about interruptions is also important. Solve the problems you can solve. (For example, buy a pump and filter for the fishbowl so you won't have to change the water so often.) Then change your attitude about the problems you can't solve. When the phone rings tell yourself that chatting for a minute is a nice change of pace. "The pause that refreshes" sounds less irritating than "interruption"!

When the kids or your spouse interrupt your activities, you can think of it as an inconsiderate act or a moment to teach, listen, and show love.

HOW TO HANDLE INTERRUPTIONS

Let's talk about some specific ways to handle these insidious time-robbers. But first you must know that time management is a very personal matter. We can't all use the same techniques because we all have different personalities. What works for one person will not work for another.

For example, I know of one man who ends phone conversations by saying lightheartedly, "Well, I'm getting tired of talking to you." Or, "I'm getting bored with this whole conversation." With his particular personality it comes off great, and he gets away with it. However, you couldn't get *me* to try it!

So, throughout the suggestions that follow, try to pick up some ideas that you are comfortable with and see if your interruption problem can at least be mitigated.

Most everyone ranks the telephone as Archenemy Number One (as far as interruptions are concerned). A lot of people take the phone off the hook or unplug it. (In preplug days, my mom used to put a pillow under her desk style phone and one on top of it!) Some folks with nerves of steel let the phone ring.

One woman I know keeps her phone off the hook every morning until ten or until her top-priority tasks are completed. Her friends soon learn when is the best time to catch her, and they call her later. She eliminates phone solicitors, bill collectors, etc. during her high-priority time. Her attitude about emergencies is that there are other ways to be contacted and if it's important enough, she'll be reached.

As you're cleaning house, you can do your kitchen last. Whenever the phone rings, answer it in the kitchen and clean as you talk. When the conversation is over, return to where you were when the phone rang and get back to your original job. If the phone rings often enough, the whole kitchen can be done in what would have been wasted time.

Another idea is to keep a craft or other project in a covered basket by the phone. Whenever the phone rings, use it as a signal to work on your project. Crocheting, knitting, embroidery, cross-stitch, needlepoint, mending, and ironing are all good phone projects. Besides, you'll be surprised how fast something can be completed when you chip away at it regularly.

We've all read lists of things you can do while talking on the phone: fold and mend clothes, iron, straighten drawers and cupboards, clean stoves, refrigerators, wipe down a wall, and do your nails (to name a few). (Telephone shoulder rests will allow you to use both hands freely while you're talking.) One important thing is always omitted from this list and that is to sit down and enjoy the call! There really is nothing wrong with sitting down and doing nothing! (It took a lot of courage to say that, by the way!) Relaxation is not a waste of time, providing it isn't your number-one priority. We all need to be less compulsive so we can savor life and each other a little more.

SAYING NO

If you simply can't say no without feeling uncomfortable, calendaring and scheduling can help painlessly eliminate a lot of problems. Many of us are concerned with outside demands on our time. Always remember that people are more important than programs and you have to use wise judgment when you say no.

Your first priority is your family and the responsibility you have to the lifestyle you have chosen. If your willingness to help others is really being abused, use your calendar. List the things you want to accomplish, and tell the interrupter you can't squeeze another thing in.

Set firm appointments with yourself to accomplish high-priority jobs. Treat these appointments with the same respect you would if it were an appointment with your lawyer. If someone calls or in some other way interrupts you and asks you to do something you feel you can't (or shouldn't) handle, tell your friend (or whomever) that you have an appointment and you just can't miss it.

Once again, here are a few miscellaneous tips to help you cut down on other interruptions.

- Have a set time for yourself and make others honor it.
- Give things in your home a well-defined place so you won't be continually interrupted to find things.

- Schedule canning seasons on your calendar so you can prepare for them and be able to work your household schedule around them.
- Plan menus carefully so all ingredients are on hand. (Hide especially tempting ingredients so they'll be there when you need them).
- Stock up on birthday-party presents, wrapping paper, and cards, and save many trips to the store.
- Hang a note on the front door when you don't want to be disturbed.
- When playing chauffeur, do grocery shopping or run other errands while the kids are taking lessons (or whatever).
- Schedule housekeeping and other projects so you'll have all your supplies handy when you need them.
- Note little annoyances and prepare for them. For example, our youngest child has a passion for milk and he was constantly asking me for some. Now, we keep a glass in the refrigerator just for him. Whenever he's thirsty he can get his own drink without interrupting anyone.

As you organize each area of your home and your life you will have fewer and fewer interruptions. Isn't it exciting to discover that a few basic organizing principles can change your whole life?

24

Where Do I Start?

"If my head were flat, I'd probably store things on it," lamented Mrs. X. "I really don't care for housework. I'd much rather read a book than scrub the floor; but things are drastically out of control! I have to *do* something! Where do I start?"

Every day I get calls and letters from people all over the country usually with the same request, "Where do I start?" To the inquirer I say, "What one area is really bothering you?" The standard answer is "Everything!"

If you feel, as these people do, that the walls of Jericho are tumbling down around you, take heart. You *can* get control over your surroundings, but you have to want success enough to exercise patience, persistence and energy. As one caterpillar said to the other caterpillar, "You have to want to fly so much that you're willing to give up being a caterpillar!" If you're ready to become a butterfly, you'll be able to do it.

DECIDING WHERE TO START

Deciding where to start is always the hardest part, especially when so many things (and people) are screaming for your attention. To find *your* best place to start, begin with this checklist:

I am able to keep the house picked up.
I am able to keep the laundry current.
Meals are well-prepared and served regularly.
The kitchen is usually in good order.
Bathrooms are cleaned and straightened regularly.
I am able to keep entry areas clean and tidy.

Before you begin any organizational project, make sure that these six areas are under control. They are the bare essentials that will keep your home running smoothly. They are the most important; so, try not to neglect or overlook them.

If several of these are a problem, the first three (pickup, laundry, and meals) are paramount. Begin with only one of them. Make your choice and determine that you will concentrate your efforts on that *one* area. Force yourself, if necessary, to keep that one chosen area current for six weeks. Try not to let any other areas bother you. For now, you will work on one thing at a time.

The principle of concentrating your attention on one chosen area worked very well for one home manager:

"For years I was frustrated and discouraged. My house was disorganized. I had grandchildren I wanted to sew for. My living room needed redecorating. I wanted to assemble a photograph album for my mother. My part-time job took extra hours from my day. There were so many things I wanted to do. Other people did them—I just talked about doing them. These overwhelming feelings gradually led to depression.

"I would browse through fabric shops looking for upholstery material one day; clean out a kitchen cupboard the next day; cut out a pattern for my granddaughter, and on and on never finishing anything. Then I tried to concentrate and to focus on one thing.

"While sewing for the grandkids I forgot about the living room. Sometimes it was hard, but I forced myself to concentrate on the job at hand. Step by step I am getting control of my life and loving it."

At the end of six weeks, check your progress. If you think you can maintain this area, choose another and go on. However, if you're still struggling, give it another six weeks. Don't be discouraged. You are probably trying to undo bad habits that took years to develop.

Think about the oyster. At first a grain of sand under its shell is a bothersome irritation. In time, however, this annoying kernel becomes a precious pearl.

If the top six areas are not causing problems and you still feel defeated, further probing is necessary. Take a minute to sit down and collect your thoughts. Make a written list of everything that's bothering you. (If you're feeling especially brave, ask your family what they would like to see changed. If they feel a part of the plan, they may be more cooperative.)

Take a look at your list and put a check by the things that are:

1. Causing a lot of interruptions. (These items are wasting your time and causing you to spend more hours on housework than you need to.)

2. A source of great irritation for your spouse or other family member. (These things are giving rise to tension and anxiety.)

3. Really bothering you. (These items are giving you "that feeling." They are making you uncomfortable.)

These checked entries should be given top priority. If many things are checked, pick one at random and begin.

Once you can see (via your written list) what's bothering you, you can get a handle on it and begin your six-week program, if necessary.

If, after using the checklist, you still can't decide where to begin, just go about your normal routine for a few days. Be mindful, though, of the troublespots that continually create a snag in your daily living. Surely you will discover something so irritating that you *have* to do something about it.

For example, after our children started coming, I began to really feel bogged down by the washing. At three or four in the afternoon I could feel this black cloud hovering over me. I still had wet clothes waiting to be dried and dirty clothes needing to be washed. My outlook was dim because I didn't want an evening of finishing, folding, and putting away the wash.

I hated the wash and I hated those feelings. I knew the wash wasn't going to go away, so I had to change my approach or be miserable for the rest of my washing career.

I decided to wash on Monday, Wednesday, Friday, and Saturday. That way, I would have three days when I didn't have to worry or feel guilty about it. Planning the days didn't help a lot, though. I was finding that after I fed the children and bathed the baby, I wasn't even able to start the washing until 9 or 10 a.m. There was enough time during the busy early morning hours to throw a load into the washer, but here wasn't enough time to sort, pretreat stains, check pockets, and turn everything right side out. So I started storing and pretreating the wash the night before.

With this system, I could have all the clothes put away by 10 a.m. When I got up at 5 or 6 a.m. I could have the clothes put away by 7 or 8 a.m. Winning the washday battle was such a triumph! I felt like I had really conquered something.

One day I went to pick up two girls who were going to spend a week at our home. Their mother was concerned that they wouldn't have enough clothing with them. She said, "You wash all the time, don't you?" I smiled to myself, knowing I was freed from having to wash all the time. I no longer had that feeling of despair in the bottom of my stomach. I felt so successful it spilled over into other areas of my housework.

DECIDE WHEN TO START!

After you've decided where you're going to start, make a firm resolve when to start. Think of getting organized as a hobby and work on that basis. Set a firm appointment with yourself. Treat this appointment with respect. Unless an emergency comes up, do not cancel it.

You'll be surprised how much can be accomplished if you only work fifteen minutes a day or thirty minutes a day three times a week. Do not overprogram! Once you get going, you might be tempted to go on for hours, but don't do it. Move steadily and slowly and maintain each area as you move onto your next area.

If you do not have a large block of time available, keep your working area isolated. For example, do one drawer in the kitchen or one shelf. Don't tear your whole kitchen apart and dig in. A large mess is overwelming and can easily discourage you. Take small bites and chip away at your chores.

I once read an ad for an oil company that said, "When you've done one thing, you've done something." Always remember the fifteen- or thirty-minute appointment you *kept* and savor your successes. Forget what is unfinished and be proud of the *one* thing you did.

As they say in butterfly school, "The harder you try, the higher you fly!"

25

The Beginning

Once upon a time there was a woman who went shopping for a new blanket. The shopkeeper showed her the very finest blanket in his shop. "Oh, it's beautiful. It's just what I wanted," said the woman. But her excitement turned to disappointment when she saw that the blanket measured eight feet by eight feet. "I'm afraid it's just too big for my double bed," she wailed.

"On the contrary," said the shopkeeper. "You need a blanket this large. You see, it's the extra yardage—the part of the blanket that hangs over the edge—that really keeps you warm."

And so it is with our homes. That extra margin of order and organization gives us the "warmth" of security and peace of mind.

In my role as a home manager, my main goal is to provide my family a tidy, comfortable home. I want to make home a place where we all want to be. Confusion and disorder drive people away. Everyone wants to be surrounded by a peaceful atmosphere.

The only way to achieve this is through organization! Yes, there are times when things are a mess, but when the underlying things are in order, surface messes are easy to clean up. When everything has a well-defined place, it doesn't take long to put things back where they belong. So, you see the chaos never lasts long and I quickly return my family and myself to peaceful surroundings.

When things are organized you can act on occasional crises when they arise. But when things are disorganized, life is in a state of continual crisis!

Children, as well as adults, feel more secure in a home that is consistent and orderly. They know what to expect and what is expected. How can we teach our children responsibility if we fail to be responsible at home?

When your mind is at peace, the time you spend doing anything is high-quality time. Think back to a time when you had control of your home, when things were in order. Didn't you have a certain peace of mind? Isn't that wonderful feeling worth having at least most of the time? You *can* do it!

Now that you've come this far you know how order can be achieved. You have your family interested and you want to do it. But there's one last stumbling block. How do you get the energy to carry it off?

The most common complaint I hear from people is that they have no energy. They're tired. They can't get up at 4 a.m. and work until midnight like "so and so" can. A truly organized person shouldn't have to.

There are, of course, many reasons for tiredness. I have read several studies about fatigue and have learned some interesting facts.

1. Tiredness is emotionally induced 90 percent of the time.

2. Frustrations, irritations, and worry drain energy.

3. The mere contemplation of work causes more fatigue than the job itself.

4. Fatigue is not always related to the amount of energy we use but to how much we dislike the task. Procrastination, by the way, adds dislike to our chores. The longer we put off an important project, the more threatening and unattractive it becomes.

5. The people who are most tired are those whose behavior and work methods demonstrate disorder.

6. Proper diet and regular exercise are necessary to fight fatigue.

The organizing system you have just learned is the solution. This system will help you reach your goals and reaching your goals is what brings happiness. And happiness is the best stimulant!

As a real energy booster, remember this thought: Energy is made to be used and when it isn't, it accumulates in the form of fat.

Now that's motivation!

Imagine just for a minute that you have a very good friend who comes to your home every day. Everytime this friend comes, he gives you $86,400. He asks no questions of you. He only requires that you spend or invest the whole amount because what you don't spend has to be returned to him. Wouldn't you spend every cent, knowing he would be back the next day with the same amount?

Well, each of us has such a friend. His name is Time. Every morning he deposits 86,400 seconds in our account. What is not spent is forever lost, never to return. It is up to us to use these precious seconds wisely. We must wisely invest them in our lives. When we waste time we are wasting ourselves.

Stop wasting the happiness and security that can come into your life. Put into action a program that makes getting organized an exciting and attractive way of life. Getting things in order not only puts more time in your life, it will put more life in your time.

Like you, I have days when I feel overwhelmed and shell-shocked. It's on those days I remember the words of Zig Ziglar: "A big shot is simply a little shot who kept shooting."

Other Books of Interest

Confessions of a Happily Organized Family, by Deniece Schofield — The author of **Confessions of an Organized Housewife** is back with this new guide to getting your family working as a team. She shares hundreds of practical, no-nag ways to make mornings and bedtimes more peaceful, store kids' "stuff," teach kids the basics of time management, and more. 246 pages, $9.95, paper

Is There Life After Housework?, by Don Aslett — A professional housecleaner shows you how to save up to 75% of the time you now spend cleaning your home by using the tools and techniques the professionals use. 179 pages, $8.95, paper

Do I Dust or Vacuum First?, by Don Aslett — Here are the answers to the 100 most-often-asked housecleaning questions, including how to keep your no-wax floors looking like new and how to clean brick walls. 183 pages, $8.95, paper

Clutter's Last Stand, by Don Aslett — In this "ultimate self-improvement book," Aslett shows you how to get rid of clutter and make your life easier — once and for all! 276 pages, $9.95, paper.

USE THIS COUPON TO ORDER YOUR COPIES TODAY!

YES! Please send me the following books:
_____ (1145) Confessions of a Happily Organized Family, $9.95 ea.
_____ (1455) Is There Life After Housework? $8.95 ea.
_____ (1214) Do I Dust or Vacuum First? $8.95 ea.
_____ (1122) Clutter's Last Stand, $9.95 ea.

(Please add $3.00 postage & handling for one book, 50¢ for each additional book. Ohio residents add 5½% sales tax.)   1671

☐ Payment enclosed   ☐ Please charge my:
  ☐ Visa   ☐ MasterCard

Acct. # _____ Exp. Date _____

Signature _____

Name _____

Address _____

City _____ State _____ Zip _____
Send to:
Writer's Digest Books
1507 Dana Avenue
Cincinnati, Ohio 45207

For information on:
- how to get a complete planning notebook
- how to get a shopping cart with clean-up bags
- how to sponsor a Deniece Schofield Organizational Seminar/Workshop in your area
  send your request to: Deniece Schofield
  P.O. Box 492
  Bountiful, Utah 84010

5576